SIX EASY SECRETS TO
PSYCHIC SUCCESS

MYTH:
MOST PEOPLE BELIEVE IN ORDER TO GIVE INTUITIVE READINGS YOU HAVE TO BE BORN WITH A GIFT.

BUT I SAY:
BEING ABLE TO GIVE AN INTUITIVE READING IS A LEARNED ABILITY.

BY DR. DAN BARTLETT MSC.D.

Six Easy Secrets to Psychic Success

Expanded and Updated for 2024
With an All New Extra Special
Bonus Chapter

"How to Start, Grow and
Succeed at Your Psychic Business
By Applying These Six Easy Secrets…"

By: Dr. Dan Bartlett Msc.D.

Published By:

Dr. Dan & Company, LLC
4187 East Graphite Road
San Tan Valley, AZ 85143
480-888-8753
www.drdanandco.com

ISBN-13: 978-0692323991
ISBN-10: 0692323996

…Important Information…

Examples of results used within this book are for explanatory purposes and do not represent results you may experience. No promise is made or implied that you will experience the same results as explained herein. Using this book indicates that you accept any and all risk and agree not to hold Dr. Dan & Company, LLC its employees, vendors or associates liable if you do not experience comparable results to any statements, testimonials or examples used within the explanatory content of this book. If you decide to attempt to start or further your business based on information presented in this book it is your responsibility. Be advised…you may not achieve desired results as presented herein. No two individual businesses will be exactly the same…intuitive businesses are based on each individual and their particular circumstances. Information in this book is based upon business acumen and intuitive and learned abilities of Dr. Dan, a Metaphysician, a Magical Mentalist, Akashic Records Practitioner, and a successful Intuitive Reader with over 3 decades of business success in the Esoteric Arts.

Contents

"There was a man who looked around…and saw in his midst much suffering and evil among his fellow humans. The man looked up to the heavens and pleaded:" God, why is there so much suffering…why don't you send help…?" And God answered…" I did send help…I sent you…"

Just for fun…I want to try reading your mind through time and space. Follow these 6 steps…and it's OK to use a calculator for this experiment.

1. Think of any number between 1 – 100…and remember it or jot it down…

2. Double your thought of number…

3. Add 16…

4. Divide your total by 2…

5. Subtract the number you first thought of…and you'll now have a new number…

6. Now…read number seven below…

"…Throughout the ages man has sought to look behind the veil that hides him from tomorrow. And through the ages certain men have looked into an oracle and seen…is it some quality of the oracle itself…or does the seer merely use it to turn his gaze inward…? Who knows what visions may come…but slowly visions do come…and the shifting shapes begin to clear…allowing the seer to look into the mists of time…"

7. You're now thinking of your new number…which is 8…!

Dedication

We've all either heard or read at one time or another that we are a spiritual Being…having a physical or human experience. And that's right…but where did our "spiritual" selves begin or come from…? And why are we having our physical and human experience…? And how are we supposed to benefit from our human experience…?

We've also all either heard or have been told that we each have a unique purpose for this incarnation…something that we…and only we can do or accomplish for our greater good and the greater good of others. Well, part of an answer to this is…if you do what you are drawn to…and do what you love to do…doing that, will serve you and serve others too…then that is a big part of your purpose.

I'm guessing there are some folks out there who don't really care about their life purpose. But I also know there are many more folks who do care about their purpose and want to find it…and some of those, like you, are now reading this. Congratulations…following your heart and doing what you're drawn to do…are part of your life purpose.

So to your quest…I dedicate this book. If you are diligent and take the process I have presented for you here into action. I absolutely promise you'll discover all…or at least most of the answers you're seeking. The answers are within you…and this book may be only the beginning for you…so here's to your glorious quest…and to your continued success.

Thank You.

To Your Enlightenment,
Dr. Dan

P.S. I'd also like to dedicate this book to my little Pug *Foozie-boy*. I know to some he's just a dog…but to me, he's like my son. He has brought me more smiles, laughter and happy thoughts than I know he'll ever understand or realize. Thank you Foozie-boy for being so much a part of my life…I love you boy…!

P.S.S. Sadly, on Dec 15, 2014…my dear Foozie-boy passed through the veil. I miss him deeply. I know he is having lots of fun playing in that magical wonderland across the Rainbow Bridge.

Introduction

"For those of us who choose to follow dreams…there's no such thing as real or permanent failure…" When I first read that way back in the 80's…I didn't understand it. I was naïve and didn't even consider the fact that I might fail at my first business attempt.

But fail I did…in a big way. I was ill prepared for what I was getting myself into. I lost a lot of time, money and effort…and ultimately I failed so badly…I ended up getting a divorce which cost me even more than my business losses…my family.

It was March of 1985…I ended up with less than a eighty dollars in my pocket…I bought a one-way ticket from SeaTac Airport in Seattle to the Burbank Airport in California…where I then lived with my sister and her husband for the better part of a year.

It was on a Sunday almost a year later…I was doing magic on the boardwalk on the beach in Venice, CA when I was chased off someone else's spot (?)…another magician came up to me and introduced himself as only Bruce…and he said to me: *"No matter how bad things seem…there's nothing so bad that can make you give up on your dreams…that is, if you even have one…"*

In that instant…I was hit like a ton of bricks had fallen on me. Here was a guy I didn't know…yet knew me better than I knew me. Then, I realized what I had read about a year or so earlier. I was at a cross roads so-to-speak…what was I going to do…? I lost everything…even my family, I couldn't even pass the hat because I was run off.

Was I going to continue to follow my dream…? Or was I going to quit and give up…? Then I remembered what happened to me when I was thirteen years old…it was 1961 in La Puente, CA.

How I Got Started
On This Path

This is the story of how I was introduced to the realm of psychic readings and was taught the basics of developing my intuitive gifts by Madame Incarna aka Sarah O'Hare.

This story was told to me by Madame Incarna (Sarah) in 1961 during my first meeting with her in La Puente, Calf…at the carnival she was working. I was 13 years old…Madame Incarna began…"I was nine years old it was a year or so after my mother passed away. It was 1915…a carnival came to a nearby town and my father took me my dolly…and my new step mother to the carnival.

I remember I loved the sights and sounds…but to this day, I don't remember how I became separated from my father. I remember wondering around for what seemed like hours…and I couldn't find my father or step mother. Finally, I walked into a tent that was filled with smoke and strange things I had never seen before.

An older lady approached me and called me by my name, Sarah. Although I don't remember telling her my name…I remember very clearly when she told me her name, she called herself Madame Morgana. She was strange looking to me…very thin, but not frail looking…long dark hair reaching to her waist…she wore dark clothes a large heavy looking necklace and what I recall as a blanket over her shoulders.

She asked me to come and sit next to her…and I explained that I was separated from my father and step mother…and couldn't find them. By then, it was late…and the carnival was closing and people were leaving. Madame Morgana walked over to the door of the tent…and called for someone. I could hear her telling whomever she was talking to about me and my situation.

After what seemed like a very long time…Madame Morgana told me that my father could not be found…and since it was so late, I could spend the rest of the night with her…and she would help me find my father or my way home in the morning…"

Well…Madame Incarna continued…"that was the last time I saw my father…I never really got the whole story…but my father abandoned me at the carnival…and I was raised by Madame Morgana…and I came to love and honor her."

"She taught me what she called *seeing through people*… and how to read the Tarot, the palm, tea leaves, numerology, astrology, doing readings by using the magic in several old books…and what she called the Magick Wishing Boards."

Madame Incarna…is the name Madame Morgana gave Sarah as she taught and raised her. Madame Incarna stayed with the carnival for several years…but worked a number of carnivals until I met her in 1961.

Madame Morgana gave Madame Incarna (Sarah) all she owned when she passed away. And Sarah continued to work traveling carnivals. I never really did learn exactly when Sarah was born…but I think she told me she was born in 1906 on February 21st…which would have made her around 55 when I met her.

She was a treasure trove of stories about carnival life working the "mitt joint" and doing readings…she taught me a lot of very special sides and secrets of the pseudo psychic realm and doing readings, and taught me how to "see through people…" When Sarah left with the carnival that summer in 1961…I never saw her again or heard from her. The carnival stayed in La Puente, about a week and I spent every day with her.

That was the beginning of my magical journey in both doing magic shows and doing readings. I wanted to be a carnival magician and fortune teller…but gave way to the premise that I should go to school, get an education, and get a job…we've all heard it as we were growing up.

I failed to follow my dream when I was younger. So, here I am now in my mid 60's…with a different but connected dream…and that is reaching out to folks like you with my years of experience and extrasensory skills and abilities. I never forgot Madame Incarna or the cool stuff she taught me…even though I was only 13…it was the best and most memorable summer of my life.

In the early to mid-1980's I did get a taste of a small part of my dream when I became a full-time professional magician in Federal Way, Wash. Even owning my own magic shop near the waters of Puget Sound, but, reality soon set in when trying to follow my dream clashed with my family life. After a divorce and losing virtually everything I owned…I moved to Burbank, Calif in 1985.

I have learned that dreams don't always have to be given up on…just taken in different directions. Besides, *"for those of us who follow dreams…there's no such thing as real failure."* My love of magic, performing, doing readings and related esoteric studies has never been far from who I really am.

Although for the most part I always had a good *j-o-b*…through the years I always had a part time business going. I did magic shows, taught magic, and I always did readings…albeit, mostly on the weekends. But my business activities were always present.

I recently retired from the work force (in 2010) and began doing more psychic fairs and I even setup a private reading practice doing readings and working out of my home studio.

After discovering what fantastic information and service an Akashic Records Reading can offer to others…I studied how to do Akashic Records Readings becoming certified, and I now offer Akashic Records readings as well as, my psychic readings through time and space via my website and email. But I still love doing table side readings at psychic fairs and at my home…the kind of readings I was taught by Madame Incarna…and I love doing those face-to-face readings and interacting with my friends and clients.

So, if you have a dream…you have much. No matter how little you may have…even if all you have is a dream. Hang on to it…work on making it real for yourself, start where you are…and with what you have. Know that you would not have the dream…or the aspiration to be, have, or do whatever it is you're seeking…if it were not meant for to have or accomplish in your life. This is a Universal Law…and an absolute promise the Universe has given us all.

To You Success…!
Dr. Dan

Important Information
to Begin With…

As you've probably noticed by now…my writing style isn't the smoothest or the most refined as you may be accustomed to from other writers. I'm a pretty much tell-it-like-it-is kinda guy…no BS, no fluff, no beating around the bush. I know my writing style will not win any literary awards…and I know my writing style may even irritate some of you…so I'll apologize in advance if that's the case. But the information I'm sharing with you…can be life changing for you. So if you can stand my writing…it'll be worth it to you.

So…there is *a lot* of valuable, good down-to-earth, and very useful information here that you'll be able to use to either firmly begin…or move your psychic business onward and upward. Helping folks become a success and move forward with their lives is part of my purpose…just like it may be part of yours…or you wouldn't even be drawn to the psychic realm.

You definitely wouldn't be drawn to this book or any book like it…if it were not meant for you to pursue this type of business either full time…or part time. So be patient…read carefully, take notes, and contact me if you have any questions. If I don't know the answer to your question…I'll get the answer for you…and that's a promise.

The "chapters" of this book I've decided to call "secrets" that I've come up with…and the reason I say secrets is because in lots of cases they are so obvious…they are often overlooked or not even considered at all by a lot of folks on this quest. So all I'm doing is bringing them out into the open so we can all be aware of them, access them, and put them to work for us.

The "Secrets" are going to be short…and to-the-point. Some folks like long drawn out explanations…but I'm not one of them. I believe in saying what I've come to say…lets learn so we can apply what we're talking about and make things happen…!

So…here we are. Imagine we're sitting across from one another…and you've asked me: *"I've always been interested in starting a psychic business…but I'm not sure of how to go about it…or if I'm even psychic enough to start such a business…how would you suggest I go about beginning…?"*

And I answer you…*"Well…there are six easy steps you can take that will get you going in the right direction…I call them my Six Easy Secrets to Psychic Success…"*

Secret One

You Don't Have To Be Born a Psychic
To Be a Professional Psychic

Think about it for a moment…is anyone really "born" to be anything…? Or do they desire to be something…? And then take the steps necessary to "become" that which they want to be. Is a successful doctor…born to be a successful doctor…of did that person want to become a successful doctor…and then did the things necessary that took that person down the path to achieve their dream and goal…?

Well, if you have a desire to be a successful psychic…? What's the difference…? You simply have to do certain things…in a certain way…that will lead you down the path that will ultimately get you there…as you take the necessary steps and actions that will allow you be what you want.

I know there are psychics out there who say they were "born" with a gift…or that they inherited their gift and they are a third or fourth generation psychic. And that may well be a fact…but I absolutely also know for a fact…there are many successful psychics out there who were not born psychic…but developed and learned how to use their innate psychic gifts and abilities to be of service to themselves and others.

It is absolutely a known and a stated fact…that we are all innately psychic to one degree or another. And that all we need to do is develop our psychic skills just like any other skill we would want to learn, use and develop. The difference being…there are only certain kinds of people who are actually drawn to the psychic sciences and who have a desire to want to actually be a psychic…and that's a good thing.

And it is easy to know who these folks are. They are the ones who "are" psychics and are actively engaged in doing readings…and they are the ones who seek out opportunities to use their skills to be of service to themselves and others. They are the ones who, like yourself, are reading this book…and books like it and learning how to develop and use their innate skills.

OK…you have a desire to be a psychic and you would like to hone your innate psychic gifts and abilities. Here is some sound, basic information that will help you to get started…

Basic Introduction to Developing
Your Psychic Gifts & Abilities

First of all…I encourage you to use this information playfully. Psychic exploration is best undertaken with a spirit of adventure. I'll be sharing with you a variety of tools that I have learned, discovered, used and perfected over time…both as a practicing psychic and instructor. These tools have worked for me…and I am confident they'll work for you as you learn, adapt and apply them to your own unique gifts and style…no two of us are the same.

As you'll discover…what you're about to learn is laid out carefully and has a predictable and natural progression. Psychic development is predictable and natural…as long as you *BELIEVE* you already have psychic abilities and remain willing to be surprised…as you begin to awaken your psychic gifts…it is helpful to recognize how naturally psychic you already are.

There Are Four Basic Phases to Begin Your Psychic Development Experience

1. *IMPORTANT* – <u>Believe</u> You Already Have Psychic Abilities and Be Open to Your Inner Guidance to Your Own Intuition…Being Open Prepares Your Conscious and Subconscious Minds to Receive Information and Makes it Easy to Learn and Apply What You're Learning.

2. <u>Expect</u> Your Psychic Abilities to Come to the "Surface…" When You Are in a State of Expectation…You Create a Positive Mind Set Within Your Consciousness Which Will Literally Attract to You Solutions, Guidance and Answers…This is Absolutely True…and it Works.

3. <u>Trust</u> What You Are Receiving…Allow Yourself to Believe the Guidance You Are Receiving by Simply Noticing and Writing Down Your Hunches, Gut Feelings, Flashes of Insight, Ideas, and Intuitions. By Simply Annotating Them You Will Add Value and Will Crystalize Your Thoughts and Psychic Learning Experience. Within a Just a Short Time…You Should Have Measurable Evidence of Just How Intuitive You Really Are.

4. it's Important to <u>Take Action</u> on What You're Receiving Intuitively…When You Take Action and Follow Through on Your Psychic Insight…Your Life Will Transform From a Mindset of "Me Against the World…" to a Mindset of… "I Am Connected to the Infinite Intelligence of the Universe…and Guided With Positive Energy in All I Say, Think and Do..."

There are Two Important Psychic Development Tools You Should Use Daily

1. Daily Meditation…Take time every day to go inward and listen to your inner voice. Just sit and relax for a few minutes…and just be. All it takes is 5, 10, or 15 minutes a day.

2. Write Down Your Thoughts and Feelings…write down your hunches, gut feelings, flashes of insight, and the ideas that come to you. Especially if you're trying to create, manifest, or solve a problem of some sort. Don't judge…don't analyze, just write down your thoughts and feelings.

Introduction to ESP

ESP stands for *Extrasensory Perception* and is the basis of the field of psychical phenomena and abilities. ESP is outside and separate from the 5 physical senses of we humans…and encompasses extrasensory abilities which comes from outside the physical…making ESP a non-physical quality of our Being.

All of the psychic sciences and extrasensory abilities are in one way or another classified under ESP. There two distinct fields of ESP in general: There are the "ologies" such as numerology…and there is the "ance's" such as clairvoyance. The difference between the two is that "ologies" are more scientifically based, whereas, the "ance's" are more based upon the actual psychic abilities (either inherent or learned) of the individual.

So…where does ESP and the ability to use our extrasensory abilities…sometimes referred to as the 6th Sense, really come from…? ESP comes from the vastness of the Aether of the Universe or from the Infinite Intelligence. Consider, there is a force, a factor, a source, call it what you will…many names have been given to it over the centuries. It has been called the Super Conscious, the Super Intelligence, the All Knowing, the Akashic Records…and other names…what "It" is referred to isn't as important as…that you know and understand…and *BELIEVE*, that "It" exists and that "It" is real.

It is where ideas come from and flashes of insight…it is where your gut feelings and intuition come from (which, by-the-way), are your psychic abilities in action. It is where the real magic of the Universe comes from. When we use our psychic abilities…we are directly in touch, non-psychically of course…with "It". "It" is within you and all around you. "It" is a part of each of us.

That's why…when you hear "we all have psychic abilities…" it's the truth because the Aether of the Universe truly is…always was…and always will be. And we are all part of it…and it a part of us through our spiritual and psychic connection with it.

There is a distinct difference between our subconscious…and the Superconcious. Our subconscious is linked to our "physical" Being…whereas; the Superconcious is linked to our "spiritual" Being. However, there is a link between our psychic abilities and our subconscious…but our subconscious is not where our psychic abilities come from.

Our brains are physical…our minds are non-physical…our subconscious mind dwells within our brain and our Spiritual Being simultaneously…thus, the connection to our psychic abilities.

The Flow of Psychic Energy

Once it is understood where our extrasensory abilities come from…and what they really are…it's easy to tap into the ever flowing wonderful and spiritual energy. The psychic energy that is within us and all around us…is always flowing…it never stops. That's why we can use our psychic energies whenever we want…for as long as we want…wherever we are.

We are part of the Aether of the Universe…which is part of the Superconcious…which is part of our Spiritual Being. Our physical brain allows us to use our non-physical mind to desire, to learn, and to cultivate our psychic abilities…and with our psychic abilities we tap into the Infinite Intelligence i.e. the Source…and thus, the magnificent flow and the magic of the Universe…and the flow of the wonderful and powerful psychic energy that flows within us…and all around us.

There are three main sources of psychic and intuitive information that come to us…1. From the Aether i.e. The Infinite Intelligence of the Universe…the Source 2. Our spiritual connection to the Aether, and 3. From our Higher Self…*Your Higher Self*…is a term associated with lots of different belief systems…but the basic idea, is that the term "Higher Self"…describes an eternal, omnipresent, conscious, and intelligent spiritual part of you, which is your real self…i.e., your Soul Self. An in depth explanation of the Higher Self is in Secret Six…

The Importance of Imagination in Developing Your Intuitive Gifts

If you want psychic guidance…simply ask for it…as you connect with your Higher Self…that magical and spiritual part of you that is forever and divinely connected with the Essence of who you are at Soul Level.

Let your imagination guide your thoughts as you are envisioning your connection. It doesn't have to be mystical …you can envision any meaningful image that you can relate to. Examples might be a star, a bridge, a rainbow…most any image that you feel will connect you with your Higher Self which is outside the physical you.

Allow yourself lots of freedom in developing this image as you imagine. There is no right or wrong way to do this…whatever you can imagine…that is the right image for you. Whenever you need guidance, imagine your connection…relax, believe and have fun in your imaginings and it'll work wonders for you as you develop and begin to have more confidence with your psychic abilities.

Your psychic abilities will always be developing…there is no finish line or final exam. The more you use your psychic abilities…the more they will develop…and so on…that's why I suggest you to have fun with this…explore, be adventuress, try new methods and different directions.

There is all kinds of helpful and useful information available to you in books, and especially on the Internet. Use what resonates with you…and discard what doesn't. Your psychic and intuitive gifts will guide you to the information you want and need…and what you're seeking and searching for that will benefit you.

Secret Two

Begin Using Your Psychic Gifts and Abilities as You're Developing Them

Confidence in your psychic abilities will only come to you from using them…there's never going to be the "perfect" or "right" time. The perfect…and the right time…is now. Don't wait to begin doing readings…do as many readings as you can…as often as you can. You don't have to charge money…and you don't have to be that great at giving readings. But you do need to start.

Friends, relatives, and…even strangers. It's easy, *but*, you should consider using an oracle as you do your readings…a method of presenting or doing a reading. This is a tool that you'll use…a psychic's tool is a deck of Tarot cards, someone's palm, or you can use one of my favorite psychic tool, someone's name and birthday.

There is tons of free information on the Internet and thousands of books out there about learning the Tarot, Numerology, reading the palm and so on. You might even have a method or tool that isn't so common…and that would be great too…! Whatever method or tool you're drawn to that you will use to conduct a reading…that's the right one for you. And it's OK to have more than one oracle (tool) to use…

I'll share with you some information you can use right away to begin doing readings and honing your psychic skill. There a hundreds of instructional methods out there about learning the Tarot, palmistry, etc…there are as many different ways to learn…as there are teachers who teach the various methods.

What I'll share with you here is some very basic…but very good, and quick ways to learn the Tarot, Numerology, palmistry etc. You may want to do further research on the various oracles I'll go over with you…and that's fine. Learn the way you're most comfortable in learning…how one person learns…may be totally different from the way another person will learn.

First…Basic Numerology & Colorology

Just about any psychic reading system can be based upon basic Numerology…it's fast, easy, simple to apply in various readings…and easy to remember. Adding color meaning can enhance your reading even more.

First...Reading Principles

The systems I will introduce you to are based upon many, many years of experience and expertise...not just mine...but from countless numbers of readers, psychics, and those who have come before us. The numbers will never lie or give false information...as long as...they are interpreted correctly and the interpretations are given to your client with fairness, compassion, and with an attitude of service and helping. With the following information...you can give sound, accurate, and honest readings to your clients.

These methods of giving readings have been in use for many hundreds of years...their origins, for the most part, have been lost to time. But, my dear psychic friend, therein lies the real secret of these methods. They've been around and used for hundreds of years...because they allow those of us who give readings...to give good, accurate, and helpful readings...based upon honesty and forthrightness.

With just a person's name and birthdate...you can give them a special and revealing reading that can include their past, their present, and their immediate future...and you'll be very accurate.

...Here's How...

These systems can be used with the Tarot, the palm, with crystals, or any number of oracles and tools. Once you've learned these systems you'll be able to give a good solid reading...and the more readings you give...the more intuitive you'll be...and the more your Higher Self will be able to guide you with your reading as you are giving your reading to your client.

Yes, it takes some time...and yes, it takes practice. But that's what psychic skills are...time and practice. First you have a system that you build on it...and grow from there.

First...the Name Reading

Knowing a person's name can be very revealing and can yield a lot of information about that person. As a reader, when you first meet someone, get into the habit of noticing how they're dressed, how they carry themselves, what type of jewelry they ware...are they color coordinated, how do their shoes look etc. never judge by appearance...just a casual observation here.

A word of caution...be careful when it comes to rings. The absence of a wedding ring may not mean the person isn't married...and likewise, if a person is wearing a wedding ring...don't assume they are married. Remember, no judgment...

For example...let's meet *Jane* a fictional person I'll use as an example. Jane is an average looking woman, nicely dressed, not too much makeup, has on a simple chain neckless with a heart on it. We don't notice any visible tattoos, or piercings other than her earrings. She carries herself nicely, we don't see any visible scars and her eye color is hazel.

Without asking any questions of Jane…we already know she takes care of herself, and likes hearts, from her name alone…we can determine with some degree accuracy, she is most likely an active person with a certain degree of ambition. She tends to be somewhat of a loner…but likes social interaction in the right atmosphere.

We can tell she can be joyful, and enjoys learning new things…she can be nurturing and a caring woman…and because she enjoys learning new things…she's full of interesting facts and information that she loves sharing.

She can become bored fairly easily…and can be outspoken at times, she is a good leader if called upon to be a leader…she's helpful, clever, and logical.

How can we possibly know all this about *Jane*, whom we just met…and have never even seen before except for just now…? This type of reading is known as a general "personality" reading. Yes, it is somewhat general but that's what a personality reading is supposed to be. All of the information came from the letters in her name J-A-N-E…

The Information Came From the Following Chart:

A – Ambitious, Clever, Leader

B – Benevolent, Blue

C – Creative, Curious, Charming

D – Dreamer, Loyal, Family

E – Easily Board, Logical, Outspoken,

F – Feelings, Finances, Takes Charge

G – Generous, Realistic, Efficient

H – Health, Harmony, Likes Attention

I – Inflexible, Imagination, Impulsive

J – Joyful, Loves learning, Helpful

K – Karma, Trustworthy

L – Learning, Social, Intelligent,

M – Manage, Helps Others

N – Nurturing, Loner, Full of Information

O – Organized, Intense, Sensitive

P – Passion, Likes Mental Challenges

Q – Quiet, Enthusiastic, Seeks Success

R – Romantic, Logical, Respectful

S – Success, Ethical, Achiever

T – Tolerant, Compassionate

U – Understanding, Makes Friends, Flexible

V – Variety, Likes Detail, Stubborn,

W – Wishful, Sensitive, Childlike   **X** – Cross Road, Theatrical, Works Hard

Y - Yielding, Good Perspective, Shares   **Z** – Zeal, Insightful, Attracts

Now, if you think this is all a bunch of hocus-pocus crapola…try it. Write down the name of a person you know fairly well…go through the chart matching the information with the letters of their name from the chart…you'll see the chart reveals more accurate information about them, than not. You'll never be 100% accurate…but you're shooting for a good 75 – 90% accuracy rate.

Now, I'll ask Jane her birthdate…let's say her birthday is July 15, 1967. What does her birthday reveal about her besides her age…? As you'll see…quite a lot…!

Basic Numerology

Numerology is one of the oldest of the psychic sciences. It is often said that mathematics i.e. numbers, is the language of the Universe. In basic numerology only the prime numbers of 1 – 9 are used. There are two sets of "Master" numbers…11 and 22. So the rule is…when digits of a birthdate add up to either 11 or 22…they are not to be reduced down to a single prime number.

Meanings to numbers and letters go way back…some say to Pythagoras about 550 B.C. and some say further meanings were attributed to Cornelius Agrippa in his work *Occult Philosophy* in 1553 A.D. Through the centuries numerology has become a mainstay within the psychic applications in many different forms of readings. Numerology is a reliable psychic science that is widely used throughout the psychic community.

So basically, numerology is the art of telling someone about themselves from the numbers in their birthdate (or name). Here's how to calculate a person's birthdate…this is a person's Life Path number for applications using numerology in a reading.

How to Calculate the Life Path Number

Back to our example of our fictional client *Jane*: Jane's birthday is July 15, 1967…each number in her birthday is added: 7+1+5+1+9+6+7=36…we now reduce "36" to a single digit: 3+6=9.

So Jane's Life Path number is 9…which tell us: She is generally a caring woman even a humanitarian at times…who holds a high degree of integrity for herself and others.

Now if you'll go back to the reading for Jane based on the letters in her name…you'll see there are solid similarities and the general information supports both sets of information…from which to base an informative, truthful, and accurate reading.

A Birthdate also reveals Jane's astrological sign…which gives even more information about who she is. Jane is a Cancer – June 21 – July 22…so she can be compassionate and very thoughtful of others…and she can also become defensive…sometimes, easily.

Zodiac Signs & Meanings

Aries –March 21 – April 19 – Enthusiastic, Strong-minded, Confident…

Taurus – April 20 – May 20 – Reliable, Forbearing, Pragmatic…

Gemini – May 21 – June 20 – Inquisitive, Caring, Communication…

Cancer – June 21 – July 22 – Compassionate, Thoughtful, Defensive…

Leo – July 23 – August 22 – Cheerful, Uplifting, Excitement…

Virgo – August 23 – September 22 – Industrious, kindhearted, Faithful…

Libra – September 23 – October 22 – Gregarious, Impartial, Supportive…

Scorpio – October 23 – November 21 – Determined, Ingenious, Sincere…

Sagittarius – November 22 – December 21 – Witty, Giving, Ideal…

Capricorn – December 22 – January 19 – Dependable, Disciplined, Leader…

Aquarius – January 20 – February 18 – Inflexible, Humanitarian, Individuality…

Pisces – February 19 – March 20 – Perceptive, Artistic, Sensible…

Her color (based on her Life Path number) is brown…which indicates that she is practical when it comes to her life outlook…honesty is a trait she takes seriously…she is purposeful in her daily activities which can cause her to become moody…and she enjoys being just a little different than the norm at times.

So as you can see…it really isn't too difficult to give an informative, solid, good general and basic reading using just a person's name and birthdate. Now if you wanted to take a look into Jane's immediate future (immediate meaning 3 to 6 months or so), all you do is add the current year to her birthday…instead of her birth year.

Example: Jane's birthday is July 15, 1967…so for her immediate future instead of 1967 we add the current year: 7+1+5+2+0+1+4=20…2+0=2, Jane's immediate future is based on the #2

So Jane's immediate future reading would be: "She'll be more in balance with her life activities than she has been of late…which will lead her to more self-sufficient directions…but she'll find herself in situations with others that will call for some tact and diplomacy on her part if she wants to achieve some of the balance mentioned. There will also be a bit more social activities for her…where she'll be able to use her new found life balance…which she'll find will be rewarding for her…and as she builds on her new balance in life, more doors of opportunity will open for her."

Now, please understand that for the example of "Jane"…the information I've presented is a *fictional* person…but if Jane were a real person…then we would be able to check with her…and ask her if anything we've said is resonating with her. Feedback in a reading is important…in fact, a really good reading is almost a conversation between yourself and your client.

Here are the number and color charts from which the information I used in our example came:

Number & Color Meanings for Readings

Number Keys:

1 = Fun **2** = Stool **3** = Tree **4** = Door **5** = Hive **6** = Sticks **7** = Heaven **8** = Gate **9** = Wine

Number Meanings:

1= Independent, attainment, confidence **2**= Tact, diplomacy, balance **3**= Self-expressive, creative, charming **4**= Systematic, order, stability **5**= Variety, freedom **6**= Responsibility, family, acceptance **7**= Spirituality, wisdom, learning **8**= materialism, money, abundance **9**= Caring, humanitarian, integrity

11 = (Master #) Illumination and Inspiration: This is a number of high awareness and practicality to carry out great ideas. Extremely capable and able to achieve greatness…(this number also indicates idealistic day dreaming and not always achieving what those with this number is capable of…must take action to achieve).

22 = (Master #) Master Builder: Those with this number have the awareness of 11…and the necessary practicality to carry out their ideas. Extremely capable and have unusual approaches to problems and can come up with unique solutions. They can inspire and motivate others and they usually peak late in life.

Color Meanings and Corresponding Number:

1 - Red=   Exciting, Competitive, Eager, Passion, Energy

2 - Orange =   Friendly, Sociable, Self-sufficient, Proud

3 - Yellow =   Cheerful, Optimistic, Wisdom, Creative

4 - Green =   Peaceful, Adaptable, Sentimental

5 - Blue =   Loyal, Motivation, Sensitivity, Seeking, Secure

6 - Indigo =   Faithfulness, Cooperation, Reliability, Nurturing

7 – Violet/Purple =   Dignified, Prestigious, Power, Spiritual, Intuitive

8 – Pink/White =   Innocent, Helpful, Humane, Looking Forward

9 - Brown =   Practical, Honest, Purposeful, Moody, Different

Master Number – 11 - Silver = Illumination, Capable, Idealistic, Dreamer

Master Number – 22 - Gold = Action Oriented, Great Ability, Unorthodox

Please keep in mind…the more readings you give…and over time the more you'll use your innate intuition and psychic guidance in your readings. But you'll always need an oracle or tool from which to allow your intuitive and psychic skills to pull from such as Numerology, Tarot cards, etc. And if all you have is the person's name…you can at least use the name information as a starting point of your reading.

You'll want to expand on the information I've shared with you here…but you now have good starting information. An easy way to learn the Tarot is to simply use the numbers on the cards with the numbers on the chart. And as you become more confident with your cards…learning the symbolism would be the next step.

The more experienced you become…the more your psychic and intuitive abilities will be honed. This will allow you to reveal more in depth information about your client where you'll be able to reveal more personal specifics about them…and give much more than "general" information.

Secret Three

How Accessing Your Akashic Record Can Help and Benefit You

Accessing your Akashic Record can benefit you in your psychic development whether you're just beginning or a seasoned psychic and intuitive. Your Akashic Record is an immense storage base of everything about you…including your previous incarnations and especially your current incarnation.

In accessing your Akashic Record you can obtain valuable and important spiritual and mystical guidance to help and aide you as you move along your path. Not just in your psychic endeavors, but all areas of your life. And all you have to do…is simply ask for the guidance you seek.

There is no real right or wrong way to access your Record…just closing your eyes and relaxing for a few moments…and "see" in your mind's eye that you are within and connected with your Record in one way you can access your Record. Once this is done…all you need do is ask your questions and as you receive your guidance…just follow through by following you heart.

You may want to write out your questions…and as you receive guidance, and without judgment, write down what you're receiving next to your question. After you've finished your session…ponder and meditate on your answers. Ask yourself i.e. your heart / Higher Self, and you'll "know" how you should proceed.

Your Record will not lie to you…it will not play tricks on you…and it will not give you false information or guidance. Here is a simple three step formula for accessing your Record…

*"You in the physical…to Your Higher Self…
to…Your Akashic Record…"*

The name *Akashic* comes from the word Akasha, which means: The "Aether…" which is one of the five elements…which are: Earth, Air, Fire, Water, and Aether. The Aether is a non-physical essence that provides the *Source* for all physical and spiritual form that makes up the Universe.

The Akashic Records are a non-physical databank or record…of the history of the Universe that is recorded within the Akasha i.e. the Aether…and it includes all thoughts…all choices, all actions of every person, place and thing throughout all of time…it also includes all past, present, and future knowledge of all that was, is, or can be.

This isn't an enchanted place of fantasy…but it is a magical place…and you can go there any time you want…from anywhere you may be…at any time you want…and you can stay there for as long as you want. Your Akashic Record…like the Aether is within you…and all around you, all of the time.

In accessing your Record you can obtain answers and guidance to every question you have or any question you've ever had…it holds a record of every event that's ever happened to you. And you can learn a lot about yourself by being curious enough to ask questions about who you are at Soul Level.

The more you access your Record…the more confidence you'll have about how to follow the guidance you'll receive. The main purpose of accessing your Record is so you can make the best choices possible for yourself…and taking the best courses of action for yourself that will enhance and serve you for your highest possible good.

As I mentioned earlier…belief and positive expectation are important starting points when one wants to begin new life endeavors. And so it is…with accessing your Akashic Record…there are three simple steps in accessing your Record.

1. Believe the Akashic Records exist…and that you can access your Record.

2. Have a valid and good reason to access your Record. The Akashic Records also reflect our intentions…even our subconscious agendas and wanting to improve your life and seek assistance in developing a new skill and acquiring new knowledge…is always a good reason.

3. Have positive self-expectancy that you will receive the best possible answer and guidance possible…<u>then you must take the appropriate action on what you receive.</u>

In learning a new skill or developing an innate ability such as your psychic abilities…accessing your Akashic Record can be of tremendous help to you…and help you to know that you're on the right path…and making the best choices for yourself…that will ultimately serve you best.

Secret Four

How to Conduct Your Readings

There are a few things to keep in mind when it comes to actually conducting your readings. There is nothing hard or difficult about giving someone a reading…but in our legalistic society there are few things you'll want to do…and a few you'll not want to do.

Things *Not* To Do

There are a few subjects you'll want to avoid when it comes to advising your clients.

1. Never give legal advice…a client might say to you: *"I was in an accident last week…and my friends are telling me I should sue the other guy…if I do, would I win…?"* Whenever a client asks you for advice or guidance concerning anything that involves any legality…here is a response you can use: *"I'm sorry, but I cannot give you or suggest to you any legal advice or guidance…you'll need to contact a lawyer or other legal professional who may be able to help you…"*

Be direct and to-the-point…and don't ever say anything like: *"Well, it sounds like you have a good case…"* Because a statement like that can imply a positive outcome for them…and you don't want to go there.

2. Never give medical advice…and especially never diagnose…a client might say to you: *"I've been having this pain in my legs…I was hoping you could tell me how long this will continue…"* Whenever a client asks for any medical advice or guidance…here's a response you can use: *"I'm sorry, but I cannot give you any medical advice or guidance…you'll need to contact a doctor or medical professional who may be able to help you…"*

Again…be direct and to-the-point. And never say anything that may even imply any medical advice or guidance from you.

3. Never give any financial advice…that includes, *buying anything*…but especially buying things like a house, car, boat, a round-the-world trip, or other big ticket items. Never advise or suggest that a client donate money to anything…never advise or suggest a client barrow money, lend money, or give money away.

Never advise or suggest a client to buy or sell stocks or any kind of investment. These are the big three subjects to avoid…legal, medical and financial advice or guidance.

Things *To* Do

Always have a positive reason to give a client a reading that will benefit them in some way. There are several subjects that are most often either asked about by the client…or subjects you should address in your reading.

Whatever oracle or tool you're using they will help give you hints and details as to how you should answer certain subjects or questions by your client. For example…let's say your client asks…*"will I get more money…?"* If the number 8 comes up for them…or if you're using the Tarot and the Wheel of Fortune comes up…these are signs of good fortune and of abundance. So you can feel confident is saying something like: *"Good fortune and abundance are indicated for you…so as long as you give positive efforts to that end…then more money is very possible for you…"*

Now, you'll notice right away…there are a couple of the subjects listed that I mentioned are no-no's above i.e. money and health. It's OK to mention money and health but within the framework I suggested like in the example above about money and abundance.

Topics That Are Most Often Asked About by Clients

1. Money = Acquiring money is always a result of providing a service or a product…in some capacity whether it's a job, selling a service or product, or bringing benefit to others in some way.

2. Occupation = Satisfying work is always a result of doing what one loves to do and is drawn to do.

3. Travel = Having a desire to move, or to go on a trip is always based on a viable reason or desire to benefit oneself.

4. Health = Always follow the instructions and advice of a doctor or health care professional.

5. Education = To seek more learning whether it's for a new job, better position, or any kind of self or life improvement is always a good thing.

6. Romance = Psychics can't bring lost love back…never advise a client to leave a relationship or marriage…positive romance is always the result of following one's heart.

Here is a list of the top 10 wants that most people are concerned about in life…so watch for clues for these subjects in your readings in conjunction with what your oracle is indicating.

1. Fulfillment…2. Peace of mind…3. Freedom of fear…4. Financial security…5. Contentment

6. Love and romance…7.Pleasure…8. Control of life…9. Knowledge…10. Happiness

Always be aware of your ethics and honesty in your readings…never tell someone something you think they want to hear. Be wary of using extremely negative words that may scare your client…words like disaster, death, terrible accident, loss of a child or other loved one.

If you're using the Tarot and the Death card, the Tower card, the Devil card, or the Ten of Swords card comes up…although these cards do indicate possible negative situations…be careful how you word your interpretations. For example…the Death card can be interpreted as an indication of a transformation…the ending of one phase of life and the beginning of another.

The Tower card can be interpreted as dramatic and great change…also, always look at the cards both before and after the negative cards…which could indicate change that has already taken place…or change that is coming.

The Devil card can be interpreted as desires that may not be in the best interest of your client…feeling trapped either by a person or a life situation or an important life lesson to be learned.

The Ten of Swords can be interpreted as someone is planning to stab your client in the back…or an end to a stressful situation…or moving forward from a bad situation leaving the pain behind.

Just be tactful, be positive but matter-of-fact in your interpretations…and choose your words carefully and respectfully. If the Death card comes up…don't ever say something like: *"Oh crap you're going die…!"* There is a very powerful life course that is called a "self-fulfilling prophecy…" and it is very real and some people do believe in it. So be careful…

Most clients take what we psychics and intuitive readers say very seriously…and there are hard core believers out there. And your reading could be life changing for them…so it is so important that you take your work seriously…and interpret your oracles correctly.

Speaking of believers…you may find that you get a client or clients…that will come to depend on your advice for everything in their life. *Do not* allow yourself to be put in that situation…I always tell my clients that they cannot come back for another reading for 3 to 6 months. If you don't set boundaries…you'll find that some clients may want a reading every week or every two weeks. So provide solid guidance to your clients…but be careful of client dependency.

All of your readings should be strictly confidential between you and your client…never repeat anything that a client says or reveals to you to someone else…*that means no one else*…not your spouse, child, best friend, and especially not to another client. You'll be surprised what some people will share with you.

If a client shares with you that they committed a crime of some sort then you'll have to report them or become entangled in a legal situation yourself. If a client shares they are considering suicide…you'll have to report that too.

Just be careful in how you handle these kinds of situations. You may never experience these kinds of situations…but if you do…seek outside professional help i.e. law enforcement, suicide centers, whatever. The worst thing you can do…is nothing.

Successful Reading Guide

1. Remember the key ingredient of a successful reading is confidence.

Confidence will come by way of doing as many readings as possible…as often as you can…for as many diverse clients as you can. That's why I advise…to begin doing readings at once.

2. Make creative use of the latest statistical abstracts, polls, and surveys.

Be up-to-date about what's going in your community, city, state, and the country…even world situations. Clients may ask you about a variety of different subjects…they me be generally concerned about war or famine, or disease.

3. Set the stage for your reading.

Profess modesty about your talents and abilities. Make no excessive claims. You are not challenging them to a *battle of wits*. You can conduct your reading whether your client believes you or not. Yes, you'll have clients come to you who will want you to make mistakes, make false statements etc. Always be a professional.

4. Gain the client's cooperation in advance.

Emphasize that the success of the reading depends as much on the client's cooperation as on your efforts. State that due to difficulties of language or communication…you may not always convey the meaning intended.

5. Use an oracle such as Tarot cards, palm, Numerology, etc.

The use of *an oracle* serves two valuable purposes. First…it lends *atmosphere* to your reading. Second…it gives you time to formulate your next question or statement. Instead of just sitting there, thinking of something to say, you can be *intently studying* the cards /crystal ball etc.

Oracles are a valuable tool and will help you interpret and help you to give advice and guidance to your client. Choose an oracle that resonates with you and that you sincerely like to use.

6. Keep your eyes open.

Use your other senses as well. Observe your client's clothes, jewelry, mannerisms and speech (but don't judge). Watch carefully for your client's response to your statements…you will soon learn when you are in tune with your client…and always engage your client in conversation.

7. Learn to be a good listener.

During the course of a reading your client will be bursting to talk about incidents that are brought up. The good reader allows the client to talk at will. On one occasion I observed a tealeaf reader at a psychic faire. The client actually spent 75% of the time talking.

Afterward when I questioned the client about the reading she vehemently insisted that she had not uttered a single word during the course of the reading. The client praised the reader for having astutely told her what in fact she herself had spoken.

Another value of listening is that most clients that seek the services of a psychic actually want someone to listen to their problems. In addition, many clients have already made up their minds about what choices they are going to make. They merely want support to carry out their decision.

Where to Conduct Your Readings

You don't have to have a storefront or a home studio to be a successful psychic reader. You can meet your clients at any public place. Just remember…if you meet a client at a restaurant or a fast food place…always offer to buy your client coffee, tea, or a soft drink and make the reading/meeting…a social and relaxed event.

Always get your fee upfront…and I would strongly advise against charging clients by-the-minute. I've actually seen psychics who have a stop watch or other kind of time piece and keep track of every minute. This is unprofessional and tacky. I often charge by the time span…that is, 20 to 30 minutes…or 30 to 45 minutes or, charge by the number of questions your client may want to ask.

And so what if you go over by 5 or so minutes…make your reading about them…not you. Make them feel good, comfortable, and valued. People will generally forget what you do, and they may forget some of what you say…but they will never forget how you made them feel.

Remember, this a business for you…and you deserve to make money from your time, advice and guidance. But the customer (client in our case), is the one that we're here to serve. With the technology available to us…you should set up an account with The Square, or the portable PayPal card processing service…so you can be paid on-the-spot with credit cards.

Accepting cash and checks is OK too…or you can even set up and allow your clients to pay in advance on your web site. But always get paid first…before you begin your reading.

You can conduct your readings at fast food places, restaurants, coffee shops, nail salons, hotels and resorts, your home, the client's home, parks, and most any kind of public place. You can rent spaces at psychic fairs, swap meets, home & garden shows and other public events. You can host psychic parties, business functions such networking events, luncheons, and Meet Up groups.

Have some fun…meet some people…be of service…and make some money…

Secret Five

How to Get Clients…Marketing and Advertising

So now…the big question: "How do I get clients…?" There are basically three ways to get clients. 1. Advertise…2. Marketing…and 3. Word-of-mouth / referrals…

So…what is advertising…Advertising is to encourage, persuade, or influence a targeted group of people (in our case potential clients) to take or continue to take some kind of action such as buy our service…in our case a reading.

What is marketing…? Marketing is communicating the value of a product or service. In our case, our ability to provide an honest, accurate (75 – 90 %) reading that will enhance our clients life and help our client via the advice and guidance we provide.

As you can imagine…there have been literally thousands of books and articles written on the "how to's" of advertising and marketing. I'll offer you here some of the information I have learned and used through the years that has helped me get clients.

Where _Not_ to Advertise

In our society…advertising in newspapers and general magazines isn't such a good place to spend your money on advertising. It isn't a good idea to advertise in "give-a-way" publications either weekly or monthly…and it is definitely not a good idea to advertise in phone books.

The reason I suggest not to advertise in those types of publications…is because for your advertising dollar…the venues mentioned do not yield the kind of response to advertising that would warrant the kind of money these venues cost to place an ad.

The best type of advertising is to point or "target" your advertising to the audience you want to respond and want for clients. So, if you want women clients between the ages of 18 to 55…target your advertising to them via where they shop, what they buy, where they live, what kind of careers and income they have, and related target information.

For example: Where they shop…with a little research on the web…you can do a search such as "where do women from 18 to 55 shop…" You'll find that pages of information come up that you'll be able to use that will help and that you can select from.

The point is…is to find publications that these women would read and look at for their shopping ideas…and these are the same publications you'll want to run your ad in too. But this is only one example. Advertising and marketing can be as time consuming and as difficult as you want. That's why some people and companies hire marketing and advertising agencies.

But if you don't have many thousands of dollars to spend on market research and agencies…then maybe you can do what many psychics do in their advertising and marketing.

Places _To_ Advertise

In our day-and-age…online is by far the best place to advertise. And the best way to advertise online is to have a website. Then, drive prospects to your website…and the best way to do that is to run a classified ad on Facebook, and / or Google AdWords. For the money…these are the best advertising outlets for the one man or one woman enterprise working out of our home.

So…here are some helpful tips on classified ads that I hope you'll find helpful. In addition, I suggest you do some additional research on writing ads that can benefit you.

What is a classified ad…? A classified ad is a small advertisement that is grouped with other ads that are like it…and _classified_ in a special section of a newspaper or magazine or a Web site.

I have found that the most important two parts of a classified ad is the headline…and the benefits the ad expresses about the product or service. By far…the most important part of your ad in the headline. And the headline should scream the most important benefit of your service.

7 Headline Principles

1. Use odd numbers: Odd numbers have been shown to outperform even numbers. Odd numbers appear more scientific and legitimate. "93% of clients say my service is better than the competition." It's more believable than saying "everyone says my service is better."

2. Keep your headline straightforward and simple: Remember the reader is going to keep reading your ad or move on within 3-5 seconds or less. The reader should understand your message (and the benefits behind it) as soon as he or she reads your headline.

3. Use strong words: They conjure up strong emotions. Some strong headlines are "I invite you ..." "In next few minutes you're going to discover..." "Congratulations!" (don't forget the exclamation point -- hokey but it works), "You've just won..."

4. Put the benefits in your headline and use "absolute" terms: "Seven ways to increase your income is much stronger than "How to increase your income." Highlight specific benefits, not simply product descriptions. **Remember, it's not about you, it's about them!** To increase the motivating power of a headline, increase the reward promised by the headline. For example, instead of "7 Ways to Decrease Your Debt," you might say "7 Ways to Eliminate Your Debt." "Decrease" is vague. "Eliminate" is absolute and is more of a benefit.

5. Create a sense of urgency: Use deadlines, like, "Respond by March 31." Notice every infomercial says "order now." They do this because if the viewer doesn't take immediate action, he or she probably won't take any action at all.

6. Market from the heart: Think about your current customers and remember you're contacting people with the same worries, problems, dreams and goals as you might have. Address the problem your reader may have…and that you can solve it.

7. Use gimmicks to beef up your headline: Studies show that an ad headline draws 28% more attention if framed in quotation marks! The ad appears much more important because it gives the impression that someone is being quoted. This makes it more riveting and more likely to be read…*"Local Psychic Helps Clients Eliminate Stress and Fear…"* Notice how this headline is in quotes…and states a major benefit.

There a lots of good advice on the web about placing ads on Facebook and using Google AdWords…so I would suggest that you do some research…and you'll find that a well worded small ad can yield big results for you.

Another great way to advertise and market you service is to use postcards. Postcards are good because you target your audience…you put your ad in their mail box…they don't have to open an envelope…they can see your headline and benefit right away…and postcards can be more personal than a classified ad.

The big drawback to postcards…is that the mailing costs and the printing costs can add up. However, there are way to cut these costs…and some of the best advice about advertising with postcards are from a guy by the name of Bob Leduc…visit him at: http://www.bobleduc.com/

Here is another helpful link where you may find some good information about moving your psychic business to success: http://www.successideas.com/

Your 30 Second Speech

One of the best advertising / marketing tools you can use is your 30 second speech. What is a 30 second speech…? Let's say you're in a casual conversation with someone…and they ask you: "What do you do…?" How you answer that question is very important…you must answer with clarity, benefits, and say it all within 30 seconds.

Here is an example of my 30 second speech…

What Do You Do…? *"I help my clients gain insight, clarity and direction to better life awareness, relationships, and success…I use various oracles such as palm reading, crystal reading, numerology and the Tarot, would you like to see..?"*

Now…after you say your 30 second speech…be prepared for a lot of different reactions from people. Some, if not most, will open their hand and want a palm reading…and it's OK to do a quick 2 – 3 minute not-too-involved reading…just make it positive and fun for the moment.

Some people will just look at you and say…"Oh…" some will start giving you advice about different things…and yes, you may even get lectured to by a dear born again Christian who feels they know all the answers on how to save humanity.

So…use your best judgment…but here is one piece of advice I can absolutely offer that will be a great benefit to you…and that is. ***Never hand out a business card…?*** Yes, have business cards…and yes, there are times to hand them out. <u>But it is way more important for you to get the other persons contact information…than to give them yours.</u>

Here's what I mean…think about it, how many times has someone given you their business card. Now, what did you do with it…? Unless you were really, really, interested in what they were selling…you either threw the card away, put in a file, or tossed it in a drawer. But in all cases, you forgot about them and their card.

Well, what do you think is going to happen to your card…? A prospects contact information is *w-a-y* more valuable to you. Once you have their contact information you can market to them as often as you have reasons to. But if you give them your card…chances are very good…you'll never hear from them again.

Here's how to handle the question from a prospect…when they ask you: "Do you have card..?" Your answer: *"Gee, you know I don't have one right now…but if you'll give me your email address I'll email you my contact information…and don't worry, I'm not a spammer nor will I share your info…"*

They'll give you their email address…so always carry a small note pad and pen with you. And when you get home, add them to your email list. And do what you said…email them a nice thank you…and your contact info. The difference of all this is…so what if they delete what you send them…you still have their contact info and you can continue to market to them on occasion.

It's a good idea to put together a contact list…and keep people's contact info…it's literally like money in the bank. If you're going to be at a psychic fair, or giving a talk, or having a special for readings…send them the info no matter how much time has gone by…and no matter if you ever hear from them or not.

There Are <u>ONLY 3</u> Ways to Grow Your Psychic Business

1. Increase the number of customers…

It's simple…no customers (in our case, clients), no business…word-of-mouth is always the best advertising and marketing. A satisfied, happy client will tell their family and friends…and recommend you to them.

There is another way to use word-of-mouth…and that is to ask your happy and satisfied client for referrals. You simply ask: "Do you have a family member or friend you think would like to have a reading…?" If they say yes…ask them for the contact info…and ask your client if you can use their name when you contact the referral.

2. Increase the size of the sale/profit…

If you're charging $25 for a 15 – 20 minute reading…increase that to $40 for 20 – 30 minute reading. The extra time in minutes is really insignificant…since often times when a reading "clicks" and you and your client begin talking and exchanging…time goes by fast. In fact you'll find yourself having to close the session if too much time has elapsed.

3. Increase the frequency of sales…

It would be great to have a reading scheduled every couple of hours from 9 AM to 5 PM…but in reality…that is seldom the case. But if your advertising and word-of-mouth referrals are working then that's OK. But if you find yourself doing only a few readings a week…then your advertising probably isn't working too good.

The third way to grow your psychic business is to have as many clients as your schedule can stand. But also, other related activities such psychic parties, psychic classes, talks on and about the psychic phenomena are things you can do to increase your frequency of sales. From each of these activities you can book additional readings. <u>Always have more than one source of income</u>.

Give-a-Ways

Everyone likes free gifts…so when you give a reading…especially at psychic fairs, have a sheet with basic information about the readings you're doing that explains a little about your reading and the information you share with your client.

For example, if you're doing palm readings, have a flyer made up with a hand on it with the various lines…and highlight the lines you've discussed with your client during their reading. Have a place to put their name and date on it…and give it to them as the end of their reading.

And here's the important part…you put your name, web address, and phone number on the flyer at the bottom. Believe me, they'll keep it and more often than not…they'll refer you to their family and friends. ***NOTE:*** Feel free to use these give-a-ways…replace my info with your info.

The following are a few examples of give-a-way flyers I have used and still use…

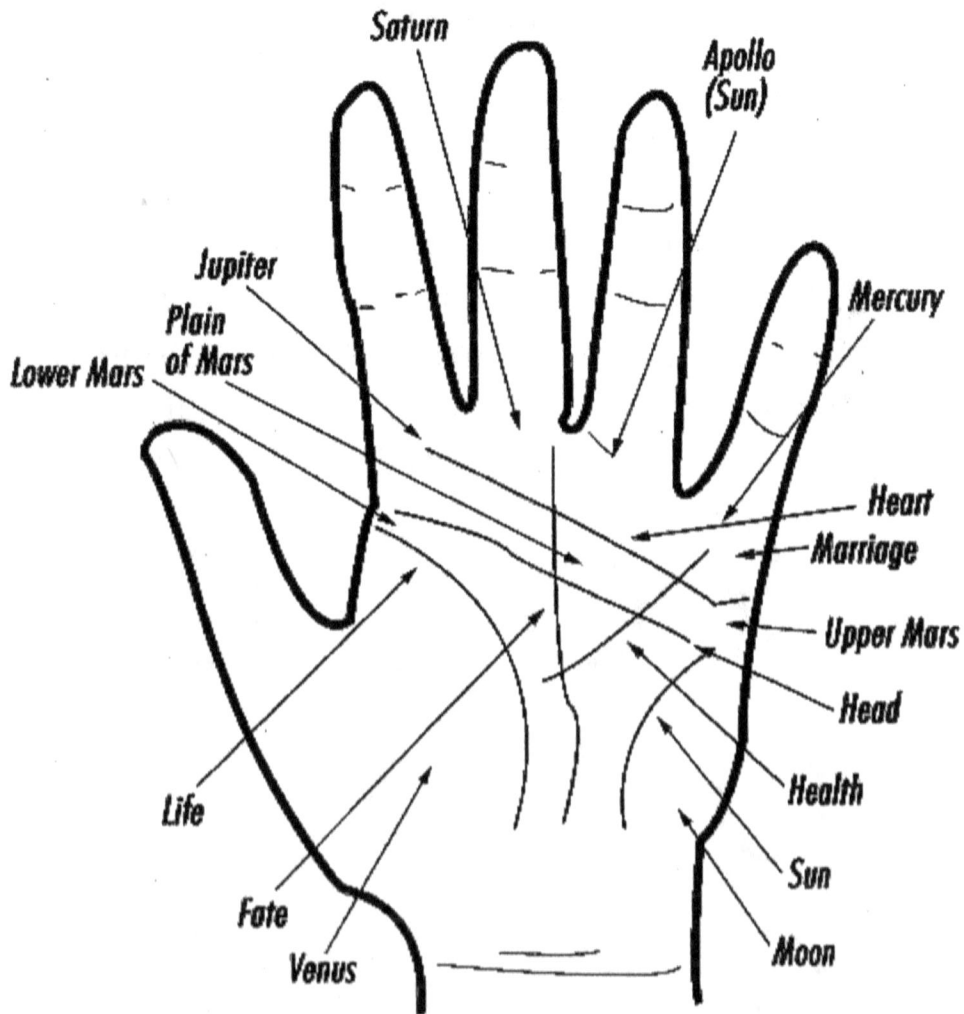

Saturn

Apollo
(Sun)

Jupiter

Plain
of Mars

Mercury

Lower Mars

Heart

Marriage

Upper Mars

Head

Health

Life

Sun

Fate

Moon

Venus

Dr. Dan & Company, LLC
Life Changing Palm Readings…*For You*
Web: www.drdanandco.com Home Office: 480-888-8753

Now, in the above example…I would, using a highlighter to highlight the lines that were discussed or at the very least, the one or two lines that the client was most interested in during the reading. Also, notice the "call to action"…the "Schedule Now", always have a motivating call to action on your advertising and marketing ads and give-a-ways i.e. "call now," "call today," "don't wait," etc…

Here's another cool give-a-way…this one is "interactive…!" Try it…

…Connect With Dr. Dan…

Follow the 5 steps below…no matter where you begin…you'll always land on and connect with Dr. Dan…Readings and Messenger of Help.

1: Put your finger on any full moon…
2: Move right or left to the closest star…
3: Move up or down to the closest full moon…
4: Move diagonally to the nearest star…
5: Move right or down…connecting with Dr. Dan…

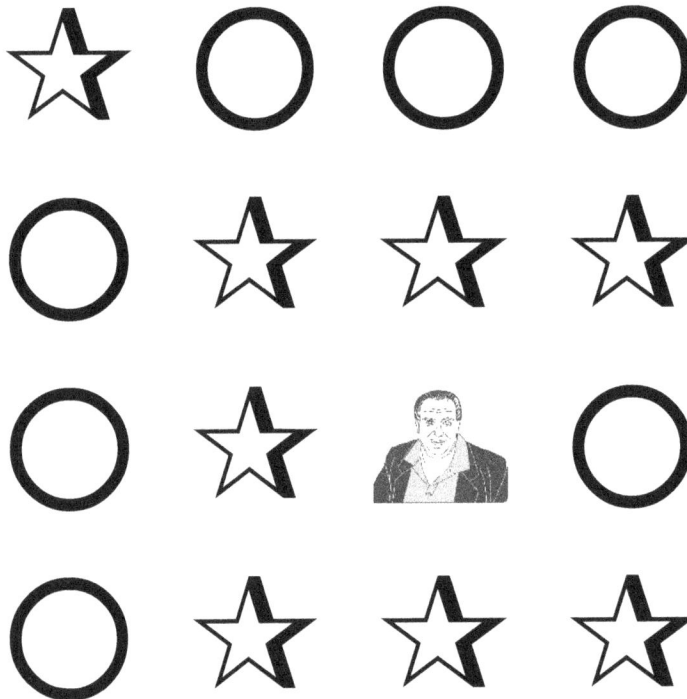

Dr. Dan & Company, LLC
Web: www.drdanandco.com
Home Office: 480-888-8753
Readings Daily…*CALL NOW!*

With this give-a-way…you're doing your clients a service…and at the same time, setting yourself apart from the some of the readers out there…Share this with your potential clients.

---

7 *HOT* Tips for Getting a Quality Psychic Reading

Don't Be a Victim of Unscrupulous or Phony Readers

1…Psychics cannot pick winning lottery numbers…so don't believe a psychic who says they can.

2…Psychics cannot bring your lost lover back.

3…No psychic is 99 to100% accurate.

4…Be leery of a psychic who asks *a lot* of questions of you *before* your reading begins.

5…No psychic has all the answers to all situations all of the time.

6…Remember to follow your own intuition…you are always your own best psychic.

7…Always exercise your free will…and follow your heart when it comes to advice and choices your psychic gives you concerning your life and future. Your future and your destiny are determined by the choices you make…and the actions you take based on your choices. Your true power is in your present moment…

Dr. Dan & Company, LLC
Dr. Dan Bartlett Msc.D.
Metaphysician - Readings
Web: www.drdanandco.com
Home Office: 480-888-8753

★ Contact Dr. Dan *TODAY* to Schedule Your Reading ★

Secret Six

Never, Never, Never, Ever Give Up

The magic of the Universe is true…and it is real. And, at the same time…the magic that is within you is also true…and it is real. Having positive expectancy and an unshakable belief in yourself are two qualities that will absolutely change your life for the better.

I was just thirteen years old when my interest in magic and the esoteric arts such as psychic readings became a part of my life. In the early 80's…I'm thinking around 1982, I began doing magic shows and giving readings professionally. Ever since my first contact with Madame Incarna, I always visit traveling carnivals whenever there's one in or around where I live.

In 1983…I remember very clearly…I was talking and sharing ideas with a carnival magician between his shows…and I shared with him my experience when I was thirteen. And I told him how I felt I missed my calling…and looked me straight in the eye…and with a very matter-of-fact tone said to me: *"Never, never, never…ever give up…"*

It wasn't until I began taking classes at the University of Metaphysics, in the mid 80's that I began to learn about our incredible spiritual and eternal connection with the Source of all that is, all that was, and all that will ever be…and how our connection with the Aether and the Akashic Records is a vast resource of information, learning, wisdom, and healing we can all have any time we want.

Once I realized that…and began tapping into that vast and wonderful resource…things in my life began to change for the better. And I began to understand life from a different point of view. Now, I tap into my Akashic Record almost daily…for guidance, learning and healing.

In putting together this book…I tapped into my Akashic Record to help me put my experience and expertise into order which I used to organize and put my information into a flow of information that I'm hoping can be easily followed by you.

In addition to the metaphysical sciences, psychic sciences, and our spiritual connection with the Aether of the Universe…there are also Universal Laws that help us as we go through our life. Just like the laws of man…as long as we do things within the law, we have no problems. Do something outside of the law, and we find ourselves at odds with authority creating chaos in our life.

There is one Universal Law in particular, that if we know and adhere to, our life can be enhanced…and that is the: *Universal Law of Cause and Effect…*

The Universal Law of Cause and Effect

There are two very simple questions which, once we understand their answers, can change our life dramatically for the better. This is so because these two questions relate to absolutely everything that we experience and manifest in our life.

Everything in the Universe is based upon Universal Laws that never error. To live in harmony with these laws…will bring to you prosperity, health, and happiness. Such harmony can result in well-being and prosperity, simply because you would be riding on the currents that build and continue all creation. Answering these two questions help us in understanding…

1. What are Universal Laws…?

2. Why are There Universal Laws…?

Once we understand the answers…we begin to see how dramatically how our life can be empowered by new insight.

To begin…consider, briefly, why the Universe exists. The reason behind the creation of creation could be summarized as follows: *"In the absence of that which is not, that which is…is not. In other words, the Original Source of all…was all that there was…there was nothing else…"*

This Infinite or Source…knew itself to be omnipresent, but without something to compare itself with…there was no way of experiencing *Its* infinity and power. The Source *lived* in a realm of absolute…where comparison, and therefore experience, was impossible.

We need something to experience…before experience can occur…so *The Source* possessed all Knowing, but needed experience to bring *Its* knowing into a completed state of Being…bringing about the so-called, Big Band…?

Now, this explanation, at this point any way…is my interpretation of metaphysical studies. It may well be pure fantasy, theory, and conjecture. But, in my mind, and belief system, there are no accidents within the makeup of the Universe…so there must be a beginning and a reason for the Universe to be…and there must be Universal Laws in place to guide all that is and to give structure to it all.

The solution for *Itself* was to individualize *Itself* into seemingly separate forms so that each of these forms could experience themselves in relation to others. Hence the realm of relativity and experience took place out of that desire to Know *Itself*…?

As we try to explain and when it is said that the Aether is everywhere, all the time…that statement has more literal meaning than can be imagined. Literally…everything is an extension of that Original Presence or Source…an expression of an aspect of *It* all. *It* creates by extending *Itself*, ensuring that all creation is in the image and likeness of *Itself*…spiritually speaking.

So this could be an explanation of the origin of the Universal Laws.

My studies have shown me that the primary purpose of creation was for Source to experience Itself. So if we observe the cycle of creation closely…we'll notice that it follows the birth-life-death cycle: *"From the non-physical, to the physical, to the non-physical…"*

Through this process, we humans come to know ourselves by materializing knowingness (thought), then experiencing thought and emotion…then choosing and converting that knowing of choice…and from choice to experience…and experience into life and life lessons.

For example…if you have never experienced happiness and I told you that being happy feels great, you would know in your mind what I mean, conceptually, but you wouldn't really complete that knowledge without first experiencing happiness and becoming happy.

The Source of all had to ensure that this cycle completes itself automatically and serves each purpose, without ever making a mistake. In other words, the Universal Laws were created to 1. Glue the system together through all those transitions.

And 2. Ensure that the knowing, experiencing, system of evolution, growth and learning works perfectly with predictable results so that all *Its* creation in all forms may get to grow and know themselves as extensions of the Original Source and purpose…no matter how long it took, and to do so within a system of free will.

To put it in another way…a Universal Law is a bond that connects all experience so as to achieve total coherence. The law that is the foundation of the Universe…is the *Universal Law of Cause and Effect.*

This Universal Law states that nothing happens by chance or outside the Universal Laws. Every action has a reaction or consequence and we "reap what we have sown."

The Law of sowing and reaping in more modern everyday language may also be known as the Law of Cause and Effect…first you must give, and then you will receive. The farmer plants corn…and then reaps the corn…nothing more and nothing less.

The Law of Cause and Effect…is easy to see its use…it simply shows you that you are an active part of all that is…and that your thoughts, feelings, and emotions have an effect not just on you…but your immediate environment. Your choices and actions relate directly to your life circumstance and affect others as well.

As we grow…we begin to see the link between our thoughts, words and actions within our realities. This leads us to better choices and to responsibility and increased care in our life direction as we take actions based upon our choices.

This law, the *Law of Cause and Effect*, ensures that through this process we come to eventually know our self as a sovereign creator of our own life experience and we are 100% responsible of our self and our life direction. It is a gentle law that lets us build our own evidence…for whatever we believe we will see as truth…until the day we step aside and see our self as a deliberate creator of who we are.

As we come to understand how we manifest into our life on different levels. We can come to understand that our communication with our Higher Self cannot be based in lack…but must be based upon our thoughts, feelings, and emotions. Then we can manifest whatever it is we are seeking…by understanding that it (whatever it is we want) already exists…and is all around us.

See…feel…and believe yourself already in possession of what you want to manifest…and the Universal Law of Cause and Effect…of Sowing and Reaping…must take place in your life.

Your Higher Self

The term Higher Self…comes from multiple philosophies concerning our Soul and our Soul Self. The basic premise concerning our Higher Self describes an eternal and intelligent Spiritual Being, who is, in fact, your real self…i.e. your Soul or Soul Self.

Who is the Higher Self…?

Your Higher Self is you…it resides within the Aether of the Universe. Your Higher Self is the real you…your total Soul consciousness. It is the you that is currently incarnated here on Earth…which really is just a projection of the consciousness of your Higher Self…your Soul.

Your Higher Self is the complete you…the you that hasn't forgotten where you came from before you incarnated. Your Higher Self is the one in possession of your spiritual essence or the plan you made for yourself before you incarnated into this life.

Where is Your Higher Self…?

Your Higher Self…is neither male nor female, but for the purposes of this incarnation…you'll probably want to identify your Higher Self with your current gender. Your Higher Self resides within the Aether…but is still eternally connected to the spiritual you…and nothing can break that connection.

Your Higher Self has access to all of your thoughts, goals, and intentions…everything you're thinking, feeling and wondering. It is the conveyor belt that goes directly between the physical you… and your Higher Self within the Aether…and your Akashic Record.

How To Connect with Your Higher Self

First…and this is important…know that you are always spiritually connected and in contact with your Higher Self through your thoughts, feelings, and emotions. But what you want to do is to *consciously* connect with your Higher Self. Doing so, will facilitate your access and help you to have a better understanding of who you are in the physical…as well as, at Soul Level.

Saying the following loud enough so you can hear your voice…will connect you to your Higher Self: *"I request a clear channel be obtained between my subconscious, conscious, my Higher Self and the Akasha…Ensure my subconscious, conscious, my Higher Self and the Akasha, are 100% aligned and connected and are working together for my highest path, purpose and good…and the good of all. Thank You…!"*

The first thing is begin to "hear" your Higher Self. Sometimes your Higher Self sounds like intuition…your "gut" feeling…a flash of insight. Sometimes your Higher Self sounds like a voice of reason, or justice, honor, mercy, or compassion.

Being acutely aware of your physical self, you can discern the voice of your Higher Self versus the voice of your ego. Your ego voice is usually fear-based. It takes some practice…but the more you connect with your Higher Self…the easier it will become.

Your Higher Self is that part of you that connects you directly to the spiritual presence that is within you and your psychic abilities. It is eternal, infinitely wise and transcends your everyday consciousness. It is in touch with the Divine because it is part of the Divine. Attaining knowledge from your Higher Self…and its depths of inner wisdom should be the goal of your spiritual quest no matter what in life you're reaching for.

Each of us is connected with the Divine. Your Higher Self i.e. your Soul Self…far transcends the understanding of our conscious minds. It's important to note however, that this is the same ability that all notable geniuses, great inventors and great teachers throughout history have accessed. It is also the place of magic and miracles in our lives. And is the true source of our psychic gifts and abilities.

Choice…Your True Power

Your true power lies within your present moment. Your power to create your future is within your decisions…each moment, and each thought, choice, or action you make or take in any given moment…that's where your power is. What that means is…in every thought, you're generating energy that is guided into your next thought. And the energy created by your thoughts, choices, and actions…dictate the direction you're taking in your life.

Your psychic gifts and abilities can absolutely serve you for your own life improvement. And in knowing this, you can use oracles and psychic tools to help you…serve others who may not know the things you now know…and you can help and serve them by offering guidance so they can live their life to the fullest for themselves…as you follow your dreams.

What Qualifies Me to Teach You About the Psychic Business…?

I have over 3 decades of intuitive experience and I am a Level II Certified Practitioner in Akashic Records Readings. Becoming certified was a positive step forward in my continuation of service and in helping people at Soul Level. From the mid 1980's to the early 1990's, I enrolled in classes at the University of Metaphysics, and the University of Sedona, earning a Doctorate in Metaphysical Science. I am an ordained member of the International Metaphysical Ministries and am also a Board Certified Pastoral Counselor and Metaphysical Practitioner with studies in Parapsychology.

In 2004, I was a University Research Associate…specializing in the study of: Man, Mind, and the Universe. My Holistic Life Path Coaching certification is through the Holistic Life Coaching Institute, a division of the University of Sedona and is recognized and sanctioned worldwide. I am the author of numerous articles, booklets and instructional information regarding using, learning, and sharing psychic, extra sensory, and intuitional gifts and abilities.

Being of Service

To serve others…and in doing so…you serve yourself…that's a really good reason to want to be a psychic and intuitive reader. Let your motivation be to help and to serve…and the money and other rewards for your knowledge, abilities, gifts, and guidance…will come to you in ways you cannot now know or imagine.

So to that end…I say thank you for reading this. But more importantly, thank you for putting into practice what you've read here. I know some of what you read will not resonate with you…and you may not believe all you've read…but that's OK, because as you move forward with your quest…you will find other related information that will resonate with you…and that you will believe and that you'll use that will build on what you've learned here.

So this then…is not the end…but:

The Beginning…!

To You Enlightenment & Success,
Dr. Dan
Summer of 2014 – Revised and updated: Spring of 2024

Special Bonus Secret

Additional Information to Enhance and Further
Your Psychic Journey

You Will Be Successful…!

Remember, by helping and advising others…you help yourself at the same time and also, you illuminate your own path with positive forward momentum. You'll be able to help and advise your clients enduring losses…you'll be guiding others in their search for a more profound understanding of their world around them…and you'll become a teacher of sorts teaching your family, friends, and clients how to experience a higher mental and spiritual connection with the Infinite Intelligence and the choices and changes that are part of, and that are possible with their lives going forward from the time they spend with you.

As stated…we all have the gift of psychic abilities…which are a universal power we can access, harness and work with. The main purpose of developing and using your psychic abilities is to help others and yourself to live a more fulfilled life. A good definition of the term "psychic" might be: To perceive and receive messages from outside of our five physical senses…and to acknowledge your abilities and to work towards thoroughly understanding them.

A Comparison of Physical & Psychic Senses

Our ability to perceive and receive messages from our physical…as well as, our psychic senses is related. And as your psychic abilities develop, your physical and your psychic senses will work hand-in-hand and as your confidence grows and stabilizes in your message receiving…your psychic senses will become your best indicators…and from which, your best information that you pass on to your clients.

Physical Senses	Psychic Senses
1. See	1. Clairvoyance - See
2. Hear	2. Clairaudience - Hear
3. Touch	3. Clairsentience - Sensing (related to touch)
4. Smell	4. Clairalience - Smell
5. Taste	5. Clair ambience – Taste (related to smell)

Sadly, although it is exciting to be living in our day and time of technological advances…please keep in mind that technology has a way of deadening our instinct and intuition. Technology forces us to rely on science and equations that can be shown as pure fact. Whereas, messages perceived and received from our psychic senses cannot be shown to be pure fact…so they must be trusted and actually lived or experienced to be proven as true or not. So, you must be confident in your abilities and in the messages you're receiving. Don't question, judge, or analyze the messages you receive…but trust that the messages you're receiving are true and that they will be beneficial to your client.

As your abilities develop…you'll become stronger and stronger in your inner willingness to accept your messages as "pure fact" and you'll share your messages with your clients without hesitation as fact. And you'll be able to advise them with an inner trust and knowledge that what you are sharing with them is the truth and is sound advice and confidence.

We all learn at different rates and with different methods…some of you will develop your abilities faster than will others. So diligence and continued commitment and dedication to your goal of developing your abilities are important. The more you use and practice your abilities i.e. in doing readings, the more and faster your abilities will develop.

In that light, let others know (especially immediate family and friends) that you're raising your awareness…so they'll know why you are becoming more and more aware and sensitive to your environment and to those around you. And above all…as stated before, have belief and positive self-expectancy in your developing process and give yourself permission to acknowledge and pursue your psychic development and endeavors.

Even More Information for You

The following pages are crammed full of additional information for you…and although the following information in some form may have been mention previously…the following can be used by you to put together your own handouts that you can give to your clients as additional information that they can use to help them as they travel their new paths.

…Special Note…

The below material is used with permission from my good friend and renowned international bestselling author and psychic Richard Webster…*Thank You Very Much Richard…!*

Life Path Numbers

1 - This person must learn to stand on their own two feet, and achieve a degree of independence. Once they have achieved this they can then proceed to become a leader or pioneer. They will find a number of worthwhile opportunities once they learn to use their talents…they are often self-centered. Color association is red…

2 - This person must learn to co-operate and get along well with others. They can make others feel at ease, and are extremely sensitive and aware. They are often "the power behind the throne" and may not always receive full acknowledgment for their input…but will be able to enjoy the satisfactions of doing a job well. They are likely to be highly intuitive. Color association is orange…

3 - This person must learn to express themselves…ideally creatively. They are likely to get along well with others because of their enthusiasms and joy of life. They have a good imagination and have good verbal skills. But they can be a dabbler of sorts. Color association is yellow…

4 - This person must learn to work within the limits they find…rather than batting their head against a brick wall. They are systematic and well organized and will generally be involved in practical, down-to-earth work. They must learn to accept the limitations and restrictions they find themselves in. They can be a plodder rather than a whiz-kid. Color association is green…

5 - This person must learn to make constructive use of freedom. They will find all sorts of exciting opportunities…and often be starting something new before they have finished the first project. They must learn not to waste time and to pick opportunities that will benefit them. They must not over-indulge in purely physical pleasures…as they need freedom and variety and travel will appeal to them. Color association is blue…

6 - This person must learn the joy of handling responsibility…particularly with the home and family. They will be the one others come to when they need help, advice or a shoulder to lean on. As a result they may find themselves responsible for far more than their fair share. They are capable of a great deal of friendship and love…and receive it back in return. They can be highly creative. Color association is indigo…

7 - This person works on a slightly different wavelength…making it hard for other people to feel as if they know them well. They have an excellent mind and good intuition. They will grow spiritually and ultimately develop knowledge and wisdom. They must learn to wait for opportunities which are not always easy for them. They need plenty of alone time. Color association is violet…

8 - This person will be involved in practical endeavors and will be materially oriented. They will want to use their organizational skills…and turn their ambitions and ability to work hard to benefit themselves and others. They must learn the pleasures that can come from material satisfaction. They are likely to achieve their goals…whether they are modest or enormous so they should aim high. Color association is Rose/Pink…

9 - This person is a humanitarian who enjoys giving for the deep joy of giving…without expecting anything back in return. They will be involved in helping people less fortunate than themselves. Whatever they do it will involve giving of them self. They are well suited to a humanitarian type of career, of course, but their giving qualities will come out somehow no matter what career is chosen. They are likely to be creative…so in some people the giving is in creative endeavor. Color association is bronze…

Master Numbers

People with Master Numbers as one of their four main numbers can be considered *Old Souls*, numerologically speaking. They have had many previous lifetimes and have already learned the easy lessons. There is always a degree of nervous tension associated with these people…which can work against their best interests. They normally succeed comparatively late in life.

11 - This person is naturally intuitive and has all sorts of added perceptions which they are likely to find hard to handle. They will have all sorts of ideas, but must learn to evaluate them carefully to make sure they are practical for them and in their best interest. They may be somewhat of a day-dreamer. Color association is silver…

22 - This person is known as a *Master Builder*. They have all the ideas and potentials of the 11, but in addition have the capacity to make them happen. The hardest thing for them to learn is how to harness their talents and energy to make the best use of them. They are likely to be charismatic and a bit unorthodox. Color association is gold…

Basic Meaning of the Colors

1 - Red=   Exciting, Competitive, Eager, Passion, Energy

2 - Orange =   Friendly, Sociable, Self-sufficient, Proud

3 - Yellow =   Cheerful, Optimistic, Wisdom, Creative

4 - Green =   Peaceful, Adaptable, Sentimental

5 - Blue =   Loyal, Motivation, Sensitivity, Seeking, Secure

6 - Indigo =   Faithfulness, Cooperation, Reliability, Nurturing

7 – Violet/Purple =   Dignified, Prestigious, Power, Spiritual, Intuitive

8 – Pink/White =   Innocent, Helpful, Humane, Looking Forward

9 - Brown =   Practical, Honest, Purposeful, Moody, Different

Feeding the Chakras

Root Chakra (lower spine, legs, feet Vitality, creativity.) Red foods - meat, tomatoes, cherries, onions, watercress, radishes.

Sacral Chakra (Spleen Chakra) (Pancreas. Assisting in assimilation. Practical.) Orange foods - carrots, oranges, sweetcorn.

Solar Plexus Chakra (Solar plexus, nervous system. Purification of liver and intestines. Helps repair skin blemishes, enriches brain.) Yellow foods - Apricots, sweetcorn, bananas.

Heart Chakra (Cardiac, heart. Healer.) Green foods - green vegetables, Granny smith apples.

Throat Chakra (Power center, communication.) Blue foods - plums, blueberries, fish, veal, asparagus, potatoes.

Brow Chakra (Higher self, spirituality, knowledge.) Same foods as Throat and Crown chakras.

Crown Chakra (Pituitary gland. Spiritual perception, power ray.) Broccoli, grapes, blackberries, aubergine/eggplant.

Keywords for the Numbers

1. Individualization, Attainment and Independence…

2. Tact, Diplomacy, Cooperation, Adaptability and Intuition…

3. Self-expression and the Joy of Living…

4. Limitation, Organization and Service…

5. Freedom and Variety…

6. Responsibility, Love and Adjustment…

7. Analysis, Understanding and Wisdom…

8. Material Satisfaction…

9. Selflessness, Humanitarianism and Universality…

11. Illumination and Visionary…

22. Master Builder…

The Four Main Numbers

LIFE PATH: This comes from the person's entire date of birth brought down to a single digit (except for 11 and 22). It represents the person's purpose in life.

EXPRESSION: This comes from the letters of the person's full name at birth, turned into numbers and reduced to a single digit (except for 11 and 22). It represents the person's natural abilities.

SOUL URGE: This comes from the vowels of the person's name brought down to a single digit (except for 11 and 22). Remember that 'Y' is usually classed as a vowel. In 'Lynda' it is classed as a vowel, but it is a consonant in 'Yolanda'. This number represents the person's inner motivation and what they really want out of life.

BIRTHDAY: This comes from the person's day of birth brought down to a single digit (except for 11 and 22). It represents a sub-lesson to be learned in this life time. This number works with the Life Path number for the purpose of directing the Expression.

Numbers Corresponding to the Alphabet

1	2	3	4	5	6	7	8	9
A	B	C	D	E	F	G	H	I
J	K	L	M	N	O	P	Q	R
S	T	U	V	W	X	Y	Z	

Meditation

I mentioned earlier, two of the most important things you can do in furthering your psychic development is: 1. Keep a journal of your progress…and 2. Meditate. So here's some more great information about meditation from my good friend Richard Webster.

Meditation

There are a tremendous number of misconceptions about meditation. You don't have to sit on a mountain top in the lotus position for a hundred years to meditate. In fact, you have probably done it thousands of times already and not realized it.

Meditation simply means "to think deeply and quietly" (OED). For our purposes, we are going to think deeply and quietly and look within. This is beneficial in many ways. It will help unlock our psychic abilities for instance. It enhances creativity, reduces stress, and reduces general wear-and-tear on the whole body.

There are many ways to meditate. It is easier to do this if you are relaxed. Relaxation by itself is also highly beneficial. Overly-tensed muscles restrict the circulation of blood, wastefully expend energy, adversely affect memory and vision, increase stress and can help create all sorts of illnesses.

Here Are a Few Ways to Relax and Meditate

1. Sit in a comfortable chair somewhere where you will not be disturbed. Close your eyes and take three deep breaths. Consciously think of relaxing all of the muscles in your body. Start

either with your head or feet and then gradually relax all the muscles throughout your body. You may, for instance, use words such as this for yourself: "My neck muscles are relaxing. I feel a nice pleasant warmth drifting all over my neck. It is drifting down into my shoulders and I'm allowing my shoulder muscles to relax". Continue right through the body till all the muscles are completely relaxed.

2. This method uses tension followed by release. Sit down in a comfortable chair and close your eyes. Squeeze your eyes as tightly shut as you can for several seconds and then relax them. Tense all the muscles in one arm for several seconds and then relax. Form your hands into fists and then relax. Some people find it easier to do this exercise lying down as then they can raise one leg in the air, hold it up for several seconds and then relax it, followed by the other leg. If you fall asleep very easily when you lie down, try this exercise seated.

3. Sit down in a comfortable chair and close your eyes. Concentrate on your breathing. Take slow deep breaths and hold them for a few moments before slowly exhaling. Do this ten times, and then tell your body to relax. You will feel all the muscles slump and you will be able to get straight on with your meditation.

4. Autogenic training. These are a series of exercises developed in the early 1900s by Johannes Schultz to teach his patients how to develop conscious control of their bodies. First, sit comfortably in a chair with your legs uncrossed and your back straight. Close your eyes and take a few deep breaths. Say to yourself, "Relax... relax... relax."

Focus your mind on the arm you use the most. Mentally say to yourself, "My right (or left) arm is heavy." Pause ten seconds, and then say it again. Repeat until you have paused and said it ten times. After this move around, open your eyes and flex your limbs.

You will find that the arm you focused on is much more relaxed than any other part of your body. Repeat this with the other arm, and then with different parts of the body. Finally, relax the whole body. It doesn't matter which method you use, just as long as you become physically relaxed.

Meditation comes from an Indian word meaning 'wisdom'. Once we are fully relaxed we can tune in to our inner being and get in touch with our Super Conscious mind. We become aware of being aware, and can get to know who we really are. In this state you may find it helpful to repeat a word or phrase to yourself. This could be "peace" or "be still" or anything else you choose. You might say to yourself:

Be still and know that I am God.
Be still and know that I am.
Be still and know - that.
Be still and know.
Be still.
Be.

Psychic Tools & Oracles

The knowledge that you now have is sufficient to help you use your psychic abilities in daily life. True, you will probably need to practice them for quite a while before you feel totally competent. However, if you intend using your talents to help others by doing readings for them it is very useful to have an oracle or psychic tool to help you.

When giving readings you will be making use of your intuitive ability… hopefully using most of the information I've shared with you. You may use your intuitive and psychic abilities to pick up unspoken questions or concerns your client may have. And you will be using your oracle to forecast the trends in your client's life. All of this is made much easier with the help of a psychic tool.

An oracle can be all sorts of things….Numerology definitely is an example. So are Tarot cards, Rune stones, Palmistry, gemstones, the crystal and so on. I know a lady who has her clients draw a picture of a tree, and she bases her reading on this. Another friend asks her clients to bring a flower with them, and she reads the flower as she helps her clients.

Which psychic tool is the right one for you? It simply is a matter of personal preference. Look at different areas and find the one that appeals and resonates with you most…I have never had a strong desire to read people's feet, for instance, but who knows, it might just be your thing. Try the ones that appeal and you will quickly discover which ones are right for you.

The Tarot

No one knows where Tarot cards came from originally. The oldest deck still in existence was made for Charles VI of France and dates from 1392. At times they have been banned, but right now they are enjoying greater popularity than ever before. The pack consists of 78 cards - 22 Major Arcana and 56 Minor Arcana. The modem day deck of playing cards comes from the Minor Arcana. It is said that a study of the Tarot will put you in touch with all the wisdom of the Universe.

The Major Arcana consists of 22 cards, numbered from 0 to 21. S.L. MacGregor Mathers, in his little book, "The Tarot", has a few sentences giving the keywords for each card of the Major Arcana.

Folly (0), the human *Will* (1), enlightened by *Science* (2), and manifested by *Action* (3), should find its *Realization* (4), in deeds of *Mercy* and *Beneficence* (5), the *Wise Disposition* (6), of this will give him *Victory* (7), through *Equilibrium* (8), and *Prudence* (9), over the fluctuations of *Fortune* (10).

Fortitude (11), sanctified by *Sacrifice of Self* (12), will triumph over *Death* itself (13), and thus a wise *Combination* (14), will enable him to defy *Fate* (15), in each *Misfortune* (16), he will see the star of *Hope* (17), shine through the twilight of *Deception* (18), and ultimate *Happiness* (19), will be the *Reward* (20), on the other hand, will bring about an just *Reward* (21).

The Minor Arcana is divided up into four suits: Pentacles, Cups, Swords and Wands. Pentacles relate to the Diamonds in our modern day deck of cards and represent money, wealth and material possessions. The Cups (Hearts) represent loved ones and close relationships. The Swords (Spades) indicate new beginnings. Finally, the Wands (Clubs) represent creativity and social activities.

Now…using Numerology, you can relate the keyword for each number to the keyword for each suit…and you know the meaning of each card.

Obviously, learning the Tarot will take some time and study…so you'll want to take it further and experiment with your cards…practice doing readings with them. You'll find getting to know your Tarot will be fun and easy.

Runes

In recent years the ancient Rune stones have increased enormously in popularity. The origin of them is not known and they have been attributed to the Celts, the Anglo-Saxons, the Norse and the Germanic tribes. Rune stones were known in England in the Fifth Century, but were being used in Sweden and Germany long before then. The word rune is derived from ru, Germanic for secrecy, and runa, Gothic for mystery.

The 25 "stones" that make up the *Futhark Runes* can be made from almost anything…small stones, silver, Fimo, plastic, wood and so on. It is suggested that you experiment with wooden Runes as some authorities claim the original rune's came from the Tree of Odin.

Each rune has a definite meaning: 1. Communication. 2. Partnership. 3. Signals. Good advice. 4. Retreat. Inheritance. 5. Strength. Good fortune. 6. Initiation. Mystery. 7. Restraint, caution. 8. Fertility. 9. Defense. 10. Spirit New interests. 11. Possessions. 12. Joy. 13. Harvest-good times ahead. 14. Links. Relationships. 15. Warrior. Love affair. 16. Unity. Home and family. 17. Changes. 18. Flow- a dream or inspiration. 19. Disruption. 20. Journey. 21. Rftnftfits - good fortune. 22. Ambition. 23. Indifference. 24. Sun - decision. 25. Destiny.

There are many variants of the original runes. Two different ones you may come across are Stick Runes and the Witches Runes.

The Stick Runes were used by ancient tribes with no written language. They consist of four flat sticks, each with one dot on one side and two on the other. They are cast by tossing the sticks gently away from the body. They must be thrown four times and the final result is interpreted. This is an example of Geomancy.

The Witches Runes are a set of eight stones. There origin is lost to history…but they have been kept alive by followers of Witchcraft through the centuries. Each stone has a meaning.

1. A male. Success. Good news. 2. A female. Changes coming soon. 3. Love, marriage. 4. Strife. Arguments. 5. Relatives. Relationships. 6. Unexpected news. 7. Luck. Happy outcome. 8. Losses. Partings. Endings.

Palmistry

Palmistry is a complete study in itself. First, the shape and texture of the hand is analyzed. There are a number of methods of classifying hand shapes, but the one generally used today is one devised by Fred Gettings, which divides the different types into Air, Earth, Fire and Water.

It is possible for a palm to have only two lines on it…but this is extremely rare. Most people have at least the four main lines: Heart line, Head line, Life line and Destiny (or Fate) line.

The Heart line reveals the person's emotional life.

The Head line reveals the person's intellectual capabilities.

The Life line denotes the amount of vitality and energy a person, has at a particular time. It does not necessarily denote length of life.

The Destiny line reveals the person's path through life.

The thumb is extremely important in Palmistry, and I have seen a number of Indian palmists who read nothing but the thumb.

Crystal Ball

The crystal ball is an object of fascination to all. By this stage you should not find it hard to use. All you have to do is sit in front of the ball, meditate and see what comes. Occasionally, you may see things in the ball, but usually it is a focus point and thoughts and feelings will come into your head while you are using it. The hardest part of the exercise is to relax enough to allow these feelings to come through.

A bowl of water works just as well as a crystal ball, so it is best to practice before buying one. If you do intend buying one, psychometrise (get a feel for it) each one you see first, to ensure that you buy one that feels comfortable for you. Once you do buy a crystal ball and when you get it home…wipe it off with alcohol…and keep in a cool place. Always keep your crystal wrapped in soft cloth or even a velvet bag.

Scrying…which is what crystal ball gazing is called, can be done in a number of ways. I have seen women in India doing it by gazing into a thumb nail. In Scotland I had a reading from a lady who gazed into a small pool of Indian ink.

Tea Leaves

In these days of tea bags…one would think the appeal of a tea leaf reading would have disappeared. In fact, it is just as popular as ever.

With tea leaf reading the sitter drinks their cup of tea…then swirls the grounds round a number of times (dictated by his Life Path number) before turning the cup upside down on the saucer. The reader then turns the cup up again and gives a reading based on what the tea leaves reveal. The very best tea leaf readers use their abilities…but it is possible to read tea leaves by seeing what shapes the tea leaves have formed themselves into, and then relate the meaning by using a crib sheet.

There are a number of books around, but I am prejudiced in favor of my "How to Read Tea Leaves" (!) Most tea leaf readers use a combination of clairvoyance and precognition, plus a good imagination in discerning shapes and pictures in the leaves.

Like all the other oracles…the more practice you do the better the results will be. Reading tea leaves is a particularly pleasant way of doing a reading as you sit down and have a cup of tea with your client first.

As we conclude…

Thank You All Very Much…I sincerely wish you much success in your psychic quests and adventures. Know that if you're reading this book and if you have aspirations of serving others with your psychic and intuitive gifts and abilities…then it was met for you to have and to accomplish…because you would not have the desire…if it were not met for you to have.

"A psychic intuitive can look down the road and see likely outcomes of actions and attitudes that are currently in motion. But at any moment, a person can make a new decision and alter the course of events. A great psychic leaves room for free will...Because we are imbued by the Universe and by Source, with the power to create…you can recreate your life anytime..."
Alan Cohn

Extra Special Bonus Secret

In this extra special bonus secret, you will learn some secrets that I was not going to share in this book…but, since I first published this book a few years ago, there have been lots of information that I've learned and used in my own practice…and I'm thinking you would benefit from being made aware of updated material.

All the information in the previous secrets is still valid…this extra special bonus secret is additional information for you that will compliment much of the information in the previous secrets.

I have been asked, since releasing this book, are psychics fake…this question arises from the information in Secret Number Two…" The Name Reading." The answer is absolutely not. However, the question: "Are psychic real." Is somewhat subjective. So, what do I mean by that…?

Think about it this way…if psychics were "real," then would not psychics be the only ones winning lotteries…since they would "know" what number would be called…? Or, what about world changing events such as 9-11, did you notice how many "psychics" came forward *after* 9-11 and proclaimed they "saw it coming."

The bottom line is…there are many good card readers, palm readers, astrologers, and other esoteric intuitives who are genuine when it comes to using their abilities. _But the real secret_…is this: Those who tap into their intuitive abilities do so using an oracle such as Tarot cards, numerology, etc.…in other words their intuition is facilitated by using tools conducive to their ability to give worthwhile readings.

Applied intuition comes with practice and dedication…we all have intuition, but there are those that take the time and effort to develop their intuition to the point where it is very reliable, truthful, and honest. But, remember, they almost always use an oracle or a tool to facilitate in their reading process.

That is why it is important to begin your psychic journey by selecting an oracle, and use it in conjunction with developing and honing your own intuition. The Name Reading is nothing more than a tool that can be used to help you give a solid, reliable reading.

Using the alphabet as an oracle for an intuitive reading is well over two hundred years old. From what I have researched…it was first used by the traveling Gypsies in Romania to give readings.

The system has been used and published by many readers, intuitives, and mentalists throughout the years.

If you want to really learn about the alphabet reading system, check out a book by my friend and mentor Richard Webster…his book: *Psychometry from A to Z*, Brookfield Press, Revised Edition 2012, ISBN: 798-86-467-0883-2

Almost all "psychics" use or apply an oracle or oracles or tools to assist them in giving readings. Their intuitive interpretation of the symbolism, colors, numbers, or other qualities of the oracle is what differs from reader to reader. And that is not a bad thing…there really is no right or wrong way for a reader to provide information in a reading based upon their interpretation of the oracle they use…because the information comes from the readers own intuitive development, experience, and life expertise, and in the oracle being used.

Honing Your Innate Intuitive Abilities

Your intuition is, quite simply, the voice within you. It is different for all of us…but we all have that small voice within us. It is not some talent that exists only for a few select people. Nor does the talent merely lie in having intuition. The talent that must be cultivated is the discipline to take the time to reach inside to yourself and to practice trusting everything your little voice is conveying to you.

The intuitive experience happens predominantly in one of two ways. First…there is the "gut feeling," which is usually a spontaneous telepathic thought or idea that does not seem to go away until you respond to it. And second…is the visual or conceptual symbol that can act as an imaging language from your voice within to give you the guidance you seek…via the oracle you are using at the time.

These symbols occur in your right brain, the imaging side of the brain. For this reason, it will feel just like your imagination. So…realize that is how it's supposed to feel, and you must learn to trust it. Which, is sometimes easier said, than done. But with practice it becomes almost second nature. That's the difference between a great reader…and the rest of us.

Guidelines in Developing Your Intuition

How to Listen to Your Intuition…That Little Voice Within:

1. When you get an intuitive impression in your daily life, respond to it immediately. What does that mean…? Acknowledge it, write it down, or you may want to do some sort of action based on the "information" you're receiving.

2. Continue building the rapport you have with your intuition by asking questions and practicing intuitive imaging throughout your day…such as:

• When you ask a question, release the tendency to systematically deduce your answer, and allow yourself to spontaneously perceive an image, a word, or even a symbol you might not yet understand.

• Make yourself get an answer, even if it feels like you are only "making it up." You are not "imagining" it. You are *imaging* what your little voice is sharing with you.

3. When you get an intuitive insight, *do not* analyze, criticize, expect, or invalidate your experience. Instead, *do* imagine, sense, and *trust* your experience.

4. Practice using directed, intuitive symbol imaging *every day*. It strengthens your intuition, and it also expands your vocabulary of symbols…symbols that flourish in the tarot, and most other reading oracles.

Intuitive Symbol Exercises

Yes/No: Think of a situation that you might like to pursue…but about which you are unsure. Create a simple yes/no question, and close your eyes. And "listen" to your little voice within…the very first indication you "feel" …either yes – or – no…will be the right answer in that situation. This is sometimes referred to *"following your heart."*

If you "feel" the answer is no…then do not pursue. Pursuing a situation that you "feel" is no…can cause chaos in your life. But, on the other hand…if you "feel" yes…then go for it immediately…the Universe likes swift action.

If you do not "feel" a yes or a no…then wait…you may need more information concerning the matter…or the time isn't right concerning that particular situation.

Applying Intuitive Guidance in Life Situations

Regardless of what life situation you desire intuitive guidance on…either for yourself…or a client. The same practice or protocol can be used to obtain the desired guidance. The following life situations are most prominent when seeking intuitive information and guidance.

Listening to your small intuitive voice within you…the more you do it, the better and more reliable your information and guidance will be. It is very simple to do and you need to do it every day.

For example…consider a relationship you have in your life. Now, relax and visualize the person…imagine this relationship…notice the very first feeling you feel about the relationship…does it feel good, warm, positive…or does it feel cool, windy, or rainy…? Do you "see" any color associated with your relationship. If so, what color…these are all informative intuitive indications that you can use in guiding you concerning this relationship. The very same methods can be used if you are giving a reading to a client…should the client have a question about a relationship.

When you "feel" or visualize a number, or a color concerning the matter at hand, refer to the numbers and colors chart in the previous chapters to give you even more information. It is all relevant, and you should all the tools at your disposal to assist you in your readings.

These are the life situations that most people would like guidance on:

Money…career…travel…health…education…romance. Along with these topics are the following: Fulfillment…peace of mind…freedom from fear…financial security…contentment…love and romance…pleasure…control of your life… knowledge…and happiness.

There is one other life area that seem to come up fairly often…and that is one's life purpose. A fun way to get an indication of what your life purpose may be…is to imagine you're in a library. This is a spacious, beautiful library…lots of dark wood trimming, quiet, cool and thousands of books.

Notice which section of the library you are drawn to…look at the books on the shelf before you. What type of books are they…you notice one book in particular; you reach for it…take it off the shelf. What is the book about…? That is your purpose in all probability…do this exercise in six months or a year from now. There may be changes that take place in your life that will change your life direction or purpose. Be open to them…embrace them. Remember…you can use these exercises to help your clients too.

Intuitive Answers to Questions

In your readings…the client isn't the only one who can ask questions…it is your responsibility to ensure that you clearly understand what your client is asking so you can apply your intuition via your oracle to give sound, helpful, and honest guidance.

There are several guidelines to ponder to ensure that you get the most accurate and inspiring answers. You can also assist your clients to phrase their questions to help the answers they are seeking is for their highest good.

Choose the more positive focus for the issue. Be specific. If necessary, broaden the question. Don't turn a question into an either/or question. Never limit your readings to predictive questions only. Pay attention to what is the likely outcome based on the present energy of the question and reading.

What can I do now to change or improve the situation…What should I focus on today. What is Spirit's guidance for me today.

Though these may seem like general questions…you could be giving helpful guidance that will forge the destiny you desire either for yourself…or your client. You could also be giving specific information that could lead to the connections and assistance that will support your, or your client's goals.

Highly Sought After Information About Answering Questions

The following information is priceless to most any reader…it will enable you to answer questions that you may have struggled to answer in the past. This information has been a guarded source for many, many years…very few readers have been privy to it. That is, until in 2012, with revised info in 2017.

My good friend and mentor Richard Webster published the secret and information in his book: *Divination Systems - How to Choose the Right Oracle for You*, Brookfield Press, 2012 Revived 2017. It is with Richard's permission I share it with you. Use it…but guard it.

The following *"Ultimate Secret to Answering Questions"* will help you build your reading practice, and help you with your success as a reader. Thank You Again Richard…

The Ultimate Secret to Answering Questions in a Reading

The following information is from an unnamed psychic reader from Washington, DC who shared the information with Richard Webster in 1990. The original source was said to have come from a famous psychic reader who used it in more than ten thousand readings.

IMPORTANT: This system basis its answers based on the first two or three words of the question asked by the client…which is a clue as to what the client actually wants to hear. Some of these questions can be answered with a simple "yes" or "no" …however, in answering these questions you have the opportunity to go into much more depth and serve your clients with helpful and worthwhile guidance.

1. If the question begins with "Will I" – the answer should be yes…but with effort.

2. If the question begins with "Should I" – the answer should be "No"…but the client really wants a "Yes".

3. If the question begins with "Can I" – the client is really saying "I Can".

4. If the question begins with "Do I" – it means the client is not convinced.

5. If the question begins with "Would I" – it means the client would if they could…but the answer should really be "No".

6. If the question begins with "Am I" – it means they want a "Yes", but they also want to hear that the situation is not their fault.

7. If the question begins with "Why" – it means they already know the answer they are seeking.

8. If the question begins with "What" – it means the same as a "Why" question. They already know the answer they are seeking.

9. If the question begins with "How" – it means they really don't care about the answer because it's not important…and / or, not important to them.

10. If the question begins with "Who" – it means the client already knows the person. (Note: This may or may not be true…in a reading you may want to explore further with your client).

11. If the question begins with "When" – the answer should be "Yes", but not now.

12. If the question asked has more than one choice – it means their first choice is what they really want…the second choice is what they will settle for…and if a third choice is asked…that is what they *Really* want…but they know they cannot have it.

As with any reading, an exchange of information between the reader and the client can almost always benefit the client…a reading should always be an exchange or conversation between the client…and the reader.

More Universal Laws and Giving Readings

The Universe is a magical and omnipresent entity…that can, and will provide us with information and guidance. There is a force, a factor, a presence that we all can tap into for assistance in our lives.

May names have been given to this substance which makes up the Aether of the Universe. It has been called the superconscious, the all-knowing, the unconscious, and even Father. I like to refer to it as the *Magic of the Universe*.

Call it what you will…but be advised it exists…and it is real, and we all have access to it. However, within the confines of the magical entity there are certain rules which absolutely must be adhered to if the Magic of the Universe is going to work for you. These "rules" are called the Universal Laws.

So, how do the Universal Laws apply to giving intuitive readings…? There are a few applications of Universal Laws that, when applied to giving a reading, will enhance and facilitate the reading…thus, helping your client with their circumstance, situation, or in answering their questions. Although there are many Universal Laws…I will only list several that would apply to giving a reading.

As Follows:

The Universal Law of Self-Fulfillment & Opportunity

This law says within every setback or obstacle there is the seed of an equal or even greater opportunity. By showing confidence in your ability to go forward and to succeed…and the more boldly you act upon opportunities when they come to you…that then, is this Universal Law in action.

…Accompanying Sub-laws…

The Law of Growth: If you fail to grow on all levels of your inner qualities…then you will always remain as you are.

The Law of Practice: When keeping and repeating and practicing over and over…you develop new habits of action.

The Law of Accumulation: The ability to keep-on…keeping-on…no matter the adversity are always lessons that we either recognize or not. It is always our responsibility to continue to learn and move forward toward our ultimate good as we have decided within our own hearts. No worthwhile effort…or sacrifice is ever truly lost.

The Law of Incremental Improvement: Every little step takes us closer to our destination. There are countless efforts during the course of development on all levels.

The Law of Self-Development: You have the absolute ability to have…be…or do anything you want in life. No matter your current situation(s)…if you take the time and effort to learn what you must learn…and to know what you must know…and to do what you must do…to achieve whatever it is you want to achieve. Then the achievement of what you are pursuing, must, come to pass.

The Law of Talent: You are a genius…and your greatest opportunities lie in the development and exploitation of your inborn talents and abilities…
Including your intuition.

The Law of Excellence: The quality of your life and achievements will be determined by how committed you are to absolute excellence in all areas of your life more than any other factor.

The Law of Courage: Seize the day…always act as if it were impossible for you fail…learn to always face your fears…and success will be assured.

The Law of Applied Effort: Any worthwhile achievement is always preceded by the application of directed efforts and…at times hard work.

The Law of Giving: What goes around…comes around…the more you give without expectation of return…the greater will be your return. This law is absolute…

The Law of Affirmation: The most powerful words we speak…are those words we speak to ourselves. The most powerful affirmation…is a visualization of what we want completed and whole…and it is always, the end result.

The Law of Optimism: Always be positive in thought, feeling, emotion, word, and action. We are always responsible for what and who we are…and for what we will become.

By putting the *Universal Law of Self-Fulfillment & Opportunity* into action in your life and encouraging your client to do the same…we become better persons on many levels by default. The more we practice this law…the more opportunities will come to us…and fewer obstacles will show up.

Many doors of opportunity will begin to open because one opportunity will lead to other opportunities and soon obstacles will become minor…and opportunities will be the order-of-the-day.

Having a firm belief in yourself and your abilities…and having an attitude of positive self-expectancy will all but ensure that this law will change your life and the life of your clients in many ways…and on many levels.

Dr. Dan's $200 a Day Challenge

The psychic and intuitive reading industry is a billion dollar industry…so why not use your intuitive abilities and your interest in serving clients with your interest in the psychic realm to make yourself extra money…or even a fulltime living…?

I have actually done what I will share with you now…I will admit, it does take some courage but it can be done…because I've done it, and on more than one occasion. I'm talking about what I call my $200 a day challenge. Here it is…

Imagine you're in a strange city, in a state you've never been to before…you don't have any money, you don't know anyone, no contacts of any kind. You're hungry and you need a place to stay tonight. Whatever are you going to do…?

Here's what…go position yourself on a bench where plenty of people are walking by. You bring out your Tarot cards and you start spreading them out as if you were giving a reading. I promise you…within minutes, sometimes a little longer or shorter. Someone will stop and ask if you do readings. Of course you say "yes I do…would you like one"…? You then give that person the best reading you're capable of…after the reading you ask that person if they would let others know that you're giving readings.

Now…while you are giving that first person their reading…other people will probably start to gather…once you have only one, two, or three people around…you're off and running. You charge only $20 per reading…and don't limit your readings to time. I know most readers charge certain amounts of 10 minutes, 20 minutes etc.…don't do that.

Just give your clients a good solid reading…you can give a good informative reading in ten to twenty minutes…but charge by time. Charge per reading. At $20 per reading all you have to give is just 10 readings…and you'll make $200. It may take you a few hours to do so…but so what. If you do more than ten…that's even more money in your pocket. And the best part is…you can do the same thing the next day…and the day after that…and so on.

I suggest you do just a basic 3 card reading…the 3 cards can answer many different questions your clients might ask, They don't have to be past, present, and future. They can be soul, life, direction… or…your client, their significant other, and relationship…or, career, status, advancement. Or any three subjects.

"Believe in the magic…and the magic will happen" …

Thank You…and May All the Good Tings of the Universe Come to You…Always.

Dr. Dan - Magical Mentalist
Metaphysician and
Messenger of Help

Dr. Dan & Company, LLC
Dr. Dan Bartlett Msc.D.
4187 East Graphite Road
San Tan Valley, Arizona 85143
Office: 480-888-8753

Among other things, Dr. Dan has worked as a magician, mentalist, and hypnotist, as well as, a writer, publisher, and a highly successful intuitive reader. All of which, were learned abilities...Dr. Dan lives in Arizona, with French Bull Dog Ozzie-Boy, and his ornery cat Lil-Key-Key.

Six Easy Secrets to Psychic Success, is fast becoming the "Go To" reference for learning how to succeed as an intuitive reader. Regardless if you're just beginning, or if you are a parttime reader, or a full blown fulltime professional.

Six Easy Secrets to Psychic Success is an extremely pleasant way to become an intuitive reader. It gives you the opportunity to help and to serve your clients with your readings.

In this book Dr. Dan provides you with six easy and easy to implement teachings that, if followed, will absolutely help you be a confident, and learned intuitive reader. Following Dr. Dan's suggestions, he provides you with an easy and fun...what he call's his; $200 a day challenge. Where you can make $200 in a day giving readings.

In this book Dr. Dan shares with you that your innate intuitive abilities are all you need to begin your psychic journey. You'll learn: How to develop your intuitive abilities...and PLUS...not one, but two extra special bonus chapters that can catapult your success.

www.ingramcontent.com/pod-product-compliance
Lightning Source LLC
Chambersburg PA
CBHW081137090426
42737CB00018B/3356